Donald Kulak

Synergy and Balance with the Natural World

A Blueprint for Prosperity, Health, and Independence

SolarWinds
Publishing

Synergy and Balance with the Natural World

A Blueprint for Prosperity, Health and Independence

Published by: SolarWinds Publishing, LLC

1-727-946-1766

www.solarwindspublishing.com
email: dkulak@solarwindspublishing.com

ISBN: 978-1-7353500-2-8
Library of Congress Control Number: 2023919446

Subjects
LCSH: Nature / Ecology/ Ecosystems and Habitats / Wilderness
Sustainable Buildings / Design and Construction
Science/Environmental Science
Environmental Law / Rights of Nature

Bisac Codes
ARC010000 Architecture / Urban & Land Use Planning
BUS072000 Business and Economics / Development / Sustainable Development
NAT045000 Nature / Ecosystems & Habitats
NAT039000 Nature / Animal Rights

Printed in the United States of America

Contents

Decentralization, Creativity, and Self-Reliance

Breaking the Corporate Stranglehold

This book shows, in detail, how built environments can be redesigned to become part of, and integrated into surrounding ecosystems, revealing a new paradigm of symbiotic relationships between building and land development with the natural world. The benefits of creatively working with natural, regenerating systems are massive, from every point of view: financial, health, and environmental,; while providing you with more independence from centrally-controlled, expensive (and often dirty) corporate systems. These designs work equally well for single-family residences, large housing developments, commercial, or industrial sites. They are blueprints for prodigious change, where buildings, man, and nature coexist and prosper—a merging of human law with the laws of nature.

Real estate and land/water management is used here as an example, a microcosm of how we see the world, society, and our place in it. What is often perceived as fragmented, separate, and random is often the result of an oversimplified version of things and events. Underneath these misconceptions, deeper cause-effect relationships exist. The realization and understanding of these relationships, and managing in accordance with these laws. leads to more comprehensive, efficient, and permanent solutions—without the typical collateral damages of high expense and environmental degradation.

Managing property in this way actually prevents problems such as flooding and land/water contamination from happening in the first place, and helps free you from the juggernaut of centralized, standardized, monopolistic control that does not work in your best interests

Indiscriminately excavating (destroying) a landscape to fit a monoculture, cookie cutter building template with no regard for topography, climate, vegetation, water bodies, etc. just doesn't cut it. It may work for a highly centralized and regulated building industry, but not for the end user—you.

Centralization has its benefits, such as economies of scale which often affords lower priced goods and /or services. But, going unchecked there comes a point of diminishing returns where the freedom of choice and the quality of those goods and services is compromised. Taken to the extreme, this leads to monopolistic control over entire industries. Centralization in the real estate industry stifles creativity and the ability of smaller developers to get into the game with more efficient, problem-solving and sustainable designs. Why do you think most every new subdivision looks virtually identical, no matter where it is—rows of houses almost touching each other, built on a barren bulldozed sites without a tree or plant in sight?

In the commercial sector, it is normally rows of one-level (very inefficient) strip stores with huge parking lots that create massive stormwater runoff. Conformity and standardization feed a system that is self-perpetuating, and where deviation from the norm is rarely tolerated, or even understood. That system includes the banking, appraisal, architecture, building professions and Wall Street, to name a few. They are all tied together.

The same holds true for water and land management protocols. Banks would much rather loan money to large developers that conform to the current building and development standardization because it is more profitable for them, and with fewer unknowns. It is easy for appraisers to get comparable sales of similar properties for their appraisal reports, upon which the banks depend for their loan decisions; because they are everywhere. Like a monolithic machine, the prevailing system spits out clone like developments, raping the landscapes, and doing a huge disservice to the people who buy them.

The prevailing perception and belief system is that building and managing our land and water with these standardized, monocultural, interchangeable systems is somehow the best we can do. That is a perception, not a reality. Information molds perception, and perception dictates people's actions and thus creates their reality. What if the information changed? What if the status quo did and does not act in the best interests of people, animals, and ecosystems? The following information may just change perceptions enough to create a reality more in line with regeneration, balance, health, and prosperity—for all life.

Do you buy into the centralized corporate message of scarcity, environmental devastation, poor drinking water, high-priced operating costs ... as just **unavoidable** costs of doing business? Or, do you believe in self-determination, self-reliance, and more efficient, life-supporting decentralized systems? Do you believe in indisputable facts and documentation, or corporate and political rhetoric?

Chapter One

Seeing the Larger Picture— Profiting Through Synergy and Balance

Once we rid ourselves of traditional thinking we can get on with creating the future.

– James Bertrand

Modern society views many things and events as random and existing in relative isolation, whereas they more often result from a series of connected, interrelated occurrences—a web of complexity that is the natural world. Our lives are inextricably linked to these forces despite the propensity to isolate ourselves from them. This is evident in the way we "develop" and manage property. The natural world affords many "low tech" solutions to most problems associated with the built environment, such as flooding, heat, wind and cold exposure, soil erosion, sinkholes, drought, etc. Nature's answers to these dilemmas are all around us. and we can benefit immensely from them. It just takes a willingness to plan building designs, landscapes, roads, etc in collaboration with the surrounding natural forces.

All of these resolutions will be explained in detail, including financial analyses demonstrating how your bottom line is affected (You will be amazed at the results), as well as the health and well being of everything living in the surrounding area.

Today's society seems obsessed the latest high tech magic bullet to solve complex problems. While these "fixes" may have benefit, they are often presented as solutions in and of themselves, with little or no discussion about other mitigating factors. They are also expensive and usually create other problems as side effects. There is a larger picture of perceiving buildings in relation to, and integrally part of their surrounding environment—a unified, interwoven whole with built in safeguard mechanisms, all working in synchronicity. This multi-faceted, whole-systems approach embraces natural systems for a more resilient and healthy environment. There are profitable alternatives to the inefficiencies of our mainstream building and land/water management that are at once problem solving, cost cutting, and life enhancing.

The current status quo is the result of a limited belief system of "this is the best we can do," with all the waste and environmental destruction being "necessary" and "acceptable" by-products. These beliefs manifest as our ravaged and depleted world while taking money out of your pocket.

Integrating the innate problem-solving capabilities of the natural world with sustainable technology and building methods shifts from waste to efficiency, destruction to self-renewal, limitation to creative possibility, and resource depletion to replenishing. This is a viable alternative to mainstream management and development practices of conformity, inefficiency, and environmental degradation. On a larger scale, extensive land planning and development models incorporating these principles bring higher tax revenue for municipalities due to property value increases. These savings can be used for infrastructure upgrades, schools, park land, local food production, etc. A comprehensive understanding of the cause-effect relationships between the built environment and surrounding systems opens up a new paradigm of prosperity, health, self-reliance, and independence.

Decentralization is a recurring theme throughout this book, while the status quo is to create more centralized control over most industries—agriculture with factory farms, power grids, storm and waste water sewer systems, universal real estate development models, etc. Why is this important? Because centralization is, in many cases, expensive and wasteful. Long transport, storage, distribution, inefficient standardized designs, and logistics all drive up costs. It also makes these systems more vulnerable to unforeseen events such as severe weather or any other disruption to long, interdependent supply lines. Moreover, centralization puts more power into the hands of fewer people while stripping authority and decision making from local communities. (See the Rights of Nature section for more on the devasting effects that result from corporate and government authority and control over local townships.)

Sustainability, on the other hand, has everything to do with **decentralization**, which addresses potential problems at the source before they even become problems. For example, typical large housing developments have stormwater sewer lines running along every street. During a storm, the water is piped to a centralized pumping station, water treatment plants or dumped directly in the nearest waterway. The sheer volume of water running off all the impervious surfaces is usually more than these systems can handle, which leads to massive flooding and pollution issues.

Localized methods such as the use of pervious pavement, constructed marshes, soil replenishing, flood/drought resistant vegetation, and raingardens can eliminate all or most stormwater runoff. (See sections on Water Management and Sustainable Architecture.) This absorbs stormwater at the source while at the same time replenishing underground aquifers. Ask anyone in the Western U.S. how valuable underground aquifers are, especially for farmers. This also adds value to your property as flood prone areas are devalued based on the frequency of flooding.

Water quality/pollution problems are also best treated at the source. Lake ecosystems can be balanced by working **with** natural aquatic systems. A balanced ecosystem creates clear, clean water, suitable for swimming and fishing. This also negates any need for herbicide spraying, which is expensive and counter-productive. An extensive study (see Lakes chapter) concluded that property values in lake communities substantially increased from relatively small changes in water clarity alone. This increased property values many tens of thousands of dollars per property.

Architectural styles were once designed to maximize building performance for local weather conditions. Shading, for example, was once integrated into construction plans before more standardized, interchangeable materials and designs took over the industry. Building orientation, adjustable outside window louvers or strategically placed trees blocking direct sunlight on windows during the hottest times of the day and year, can lower a/c costs by 50% or more. The same can be said for designs that mitigate effects of cold winter winds, thus substantially reducing heating costs. HVAC industry lobbyists, however, made sure that buildings became increasingly standardized and more dependent on air conditioning and heating. We need to expand our image of man, buildings and environment to take into account the complex interrelationships that exist. The financial and health benefits are many, not to mention more environmental integrity and balance.

The obvious question is, why aren't these principles being embraced by mainstream building, management and development? Because conformity and standardization fuels a monopolized system of centralization and control. This limits choices over how you live and what you pay. That is to say, becoming almost entirely dependent on standardized building templates and infrastructure that, for the most part, are outdated, inefficient, and in need of repair.

Another explanation may be that the public has been indoctrinated by the hype of the building, energy, and HVAC industries—that total reliance on technology and separation from the natural world is best for you. Also feeding this delusion is the fear-based excuse that human beings are alone, and separate from nature, thus creating anxiety and uncertainty about it. It is this perception that also furthers the rampant exploitation and destruction of the biosphere—in the name of security.

Indigenous cultures see man as part of, and integrated with nature, which results in a deep understanding and respect for the forces around them. They work **with** those forces and benefit from doing so. The current paradigm of blatant disregard for the natural world can change right now and help set us on a new course toward more self-reliance, independence, profit, and true democracy for all life.

Putting Ideas Into Action

This culmination of extensive interviews and research was written for people willing to implement and actualize this information, and receive all the benefits from doing so. This will most likely be happening from the ground up—individual property owners, managers, tenants, etc. who want to change direction from waste and pollution to sustainability and profit.

My discussions with architects and land planners examined new designs, materials, and construction methods that make buildings more efficient, durable, and resilient to severe weather. At the conclusion of these interviews, one question invariable arose. That is, if all we have discussed carries with it so many benefits, why aren't they used in mainstream building and development? The response was that builders are very slow to change and are looking for the quickest paycheck from their developments—in and out, then on to the next project. They don't want to be bothered learning new methods when the status quo has served them relatively well for so many years. Many architects agree that most builders are behind the times in implementing new designs, materials and methodologies.

There is also the perceived lack of data or outright unwillingness to study the facts that substantiate all the benefits. Then there is the centralization of entire industries where standardization facilitates and encourages development models familiar to banks, appraisers, real estate brokers, planning/zoning boards, engineers, etc. These projects are pushed through the system with relative ease, as everyone is on the same page and knows what to expect. Any deviation from this rigid model creates a whole lot of red tape, variance applications, special hearings, etc.

You, by virtue of the fact you are even reading this, can see opportunities, and are willing to act on them. You are resourceful, creative, independent-minded, and do not wait for governments to "bail you out." If enough people act, beginning with their own property, a critical mass will eventually be reached, leading the way towards mainstream acceptance and application.

The world is becoming obsessed with and ever dependent on technology. Society in general seems to have a blind acceptance for every new, shiny technological device. If something is not "smart" tech then it is often perceived as somehow inferior. That is a common perception today, but has very little basis in fact. Technology is great, but only if used to complement, not exclude, the surrounding natural forces; to integrate with and emulate ecosystem designs and functions for more resilience, balance and efficiency.

Viewed as an integrated whole, and with accurate information and data, the best decisions with regard to profit, health, and environmental integrity should become obvious. This puts you in control over your situations and not in a reactionary mode to corporate marketing hype.

The way in which we treat the ecosystems around us is a microcosm of how we identify with the world. The biosphere is a complex system of perpetual movement and cause-effect associations, where everything is connected and related on some level—including ourselves. That said, mainstream building, management and development models seem to be operating in relative isolation, imposing standardized designs on diverse landscapes, rather than working in concert with a highly valuable partner—the surrounding ecosystems.

The larger theme is one of decentralization, which leads to more self-reliance, synergy and balance. This means expanding your perception of the built environment in relation to the natural world. Of course it is much easier to just go along with whatever the mainstream media and Madison Avenue suggest you do. You don't have to think too much, just conform and do what your neighbors are doing, Don't ask too many questions at the planning board meetings because the local politicians know what is best for your community, right? They may say it will create jobs and prosperity by building a new shopping center over an existing wetland or forest. But what they are not telling you is that most of the corporate profits from such a development are going to out of state headquarters. What they are also not telling you is that it is usually more profitable for the community if other more downtown areas were retrofitted to accommodate these businesses. This would mean more tax revenue while at the same time preserving valuable forest or other natural areas. Read much more about this with detailed case studies in the Land Planning and Development section. The current paradigm is not one of life enhancement, but rather destruction.

Ask yourself what is best for my area? Try to look beyond the existing protocols and methods which have become so ingrained in our society and which have molded our perceptions as to the way things should be done.. Look at your building(s), the surrounding areas—land, water, ecosystems, or just concrete. If there are problems such as flooding, poor insulation from heat/cold, pollution, etc. open up to all possibilities beyond the rigid conventions of the status quo. Many times there are more effective, cost-cutting, resilient and life/health enhancing solutions at your disposal. They become clear if you have an open mind, observe what is in the immediate vicinity, and look for synergistic opportunities. The remainder of this book will provide you with specific methods, case studies, and a broader perspective where practical, effective solutions are revealed.

Chapter Two

There Are No Problems – Only Bad Management

Look deep into nature, and then you will understand everything better.

– Albert Einstein

Humanity appears to be at war with the natural world, the world upon which our very survival depends. Oil extraction (most notably fracking) poisons our water; large corporations are positioning to own and control the world's food and water supplies; waterways are used as cesspools and garbage dumps, natural resilient, balancing systems are indiscriminately bulldozed and paved over, etc. Many people of the industrialized world have no deep attachment to the land, and disrespectfully regard it as something to be exploited and conquered. This is counterintuitive, wasteful, and destructive.

Conversely, indigenous cultures see themselves as part of a larger whole, with all life and the entire world being natural extensions of themselves. Albert Einstein said,

> "Human beings ... experiences himself, his thoughts and feelings as something separate from the rest, a kind of optical

> delusion of his consciousness. This delusion is a kind of prison for us ."

This perceptual prison disconnects us from our surrounding environment, resulting in a false sense of isolation and a need to dominate. The trend of reckless destruction and control can be reversed by embracing the complexity, interrelatedness, and efficiency of natural systems. Effective property management and development can be used as a means to help restore balance and health to the world's ecosystems and resources, while affording more autonomy, freedom, and monetary gain for the people involved.

Real estate provides an opportunity for massive change, as most everyone is involved with it on some level—ownership, management, tenants working creatively with landlords, land use/zoning officials, land rights organizations.... Millions of people could create a shift to a more balanced and equitable system. When Mahatma Ghandi was asked how he was going to fight against the colonization of India, he just sat down at a spinning wheel and began to weave. He later said that hundreds of millions of people have spinning wheels, and that there is power in these numbers. Using the spinning wheel could put the Indian people in control of an entire industry, help eliminate English control, and ultimately regain sovereignty. Real estate can be the modern day spinning wheel.

The late historian Howard Zinn said that the best way to understand current affairs and to solve today's problems is to know the history behind them. History reveals how certain problems arose and the manner in which they were resolved, or not. It demonstrates how certain destructive patterns of behavior appear repeatedly as an endless loop, and how certain myths are reinforced through perpetual repetition until they are accepted as truth.

There are lies and propaganda that have become "acceptable" in this society, just as we have "acceptable" amounts of radioactive waste, arsenic, lead, or mercury ... that can be "legally" dumped into the air, water, and food supplies. It is the cost of doing business, economic development, and progress. That is to say, the population has "accepted" disease, contamination, and premature death as a necessary cost of living in a modern society. Until this is **unacceptable**, nothing will change. It's business as usual with blind trust in political and corporate leaders to look after the peoples' best interests.

Water-related problems are a big concern these days. There is either too much of it through flooding, too little through drought, or it's simply contaminated. There are corporate buy-ups of water supplies worldwide to commodify this essential natural resource for profit. Most of the water is dirty. All this has become "acceptable" in today's society. There's a way out of this seemingly futile situation using low/no cost solutions which reduce/eliminate dirty stormwater runoff, replenish aquifers and cut/eliminate irrigation costs—all of which can be implemented by you, right now, while profiting from doing so.

Renewable energy and energy saving dominates the headlines these days, and the mainstream solutions typically involve buying over-hyped new technology to save on energy bills. While some may be good, there are many others with long payback periods and negative returns on investment. Before investing, more effective and far less costly methods should be considered, such as methods that incorporate the surrounding landscape into the equation. To wit: A single shade tree or large bush strategically placed near a window to block the summer sun during the hottest time of the day could save well over 25% on energy bills alone. The calculations for optimal tree placement can be found in the Land Management chapter.

Conventional construction is often profligate and inept. It places little to no importance on local climate, topography, vegetation, soil type or water supplies. Large tracts of land are commonly clear cut and bulldozed to make way for obtrusive boxes that bake in the sun and/or take the brunt of ice-cold north winds, wasting billions of dollars in heat/air-conditioning costs. During storms, water pours off these barren landscapes, collects all types of contaminates, and empties into storm drains, most of which are connected to sewage disposal systems. These are quick to overload during storms, and often end up dumping sludge into local waterways or entire neighborhoods.

What happened to creative site management and construction? Innovative managers use everything at their disposal, including incorporating the unique features of the surrounding landscape into building design decisions, This can turn problems into solutions. For example, a hilly area near a major highway may at first present road noise issues and terrain requiring major excavation. A business that requires complete silence in one or two rooms such as a recording studio, but also requires the exposure of a main road could be creatively built utilizing the unique landscape. Part of the building needing complete silence could be built into a hill side using earth-sheltered construction. This is excellent for sound and weather insulation, and eliminates major excavation costs of removing an entire hill. If no hill exists, then excess dirt from normal ground leveling and foundation digging could be put to use.

What about the ecosystems of the world upon which we depend for our very survival? The wanton destruction to these intricate systems is rapidly degrading our quality of life and resources. They are living beings in and of themselves, and contain a complex interrelated web of plant, aquatic and animal life, down to the tiniest microorganism. Our society of specialization and classification refutes the existence of ecosystems as living beings, but rather dissects them into long lists of separate and distinct life forms. Other cultures see all things alive and interconnected—mountains, lakes, rivers, marshes ... all are alive in their own right. Brain scientist Jill Bolte Taylor wrote, in a near death experience, about perceiving no clear boundaries between her body and the surrounding environment, as it all merged into one unified whole. Read more on this in the Wisdom of Indigenous Cultures chapter.

If ecosystems are alive, but have no rights, they are like the slaves of the 19th century. Eventually the slaves went from an owner's property to free individuals. It sounded ludicrous back then, just as giving the ecosystems of the world legal rights to exist and flourish sounds today. If this were the case, and it is slowly working its way into our own legal system, construction and land use/management policies would drastically change. Legal courses of action are being taken by townships, cities and countries around the world, providing enforceable rights to ecosystems, the health of which are directly proportional to the health of the economy. Some cases were upheld in the higher courts, but many others were not. It remains a continuing battle of communities and townships taking back their rights to local self governance and out of the hands of corporate control.

Real estate is characteristically "valued" by the return on investment—how much extra money, or profit will be acquired through a given real estate transaction. Professional real estate appraisals place a value on property based on its "highest and best use." This is the "best use" which provides the "highest" monetary return for the **owner**, with little regard for the immediate and surrounding areas or long-term financial impact on those areas. Real estate ownership, by definition, enables the systematic exploitation of land for short-term profit. The point is that it doesn't have to be either or—the gain of one at the expense of others—profit over the environment. Seeing the larger picture, reveals how buildings and landscapes are intertwined with symbiotic, cause-effect relationships that can be used for problem-solving, profit-generating real estate.

Today, there is incessant talk of green buildings, the green economy, green materials etc., yet there are no substantive changes. One just has to look at mainstream construction practices today, as mentioned earlier. The absence of shading or wind mitigation, natural stormwater absorption, etc., results in higher utility costs for property owners, aquifer depletion, pollution, and higher taxes. This is not only inept, it also creates more dependence on centralized systems. As Ghandi once said, "To the extent you are dependent, you are slaves."

The rules of the game need to change. The current rules exploit the natural world for the "highest" short-term monetary gain —an overly simplistic and nearsighted approach with virtually no regard for interconnected systems and the creation of real wealth, which is directly related to the health and abundance of its natural resources. That being said, the party line continually repeats that whatever is good for the economy (albeit short term) is good for you. Using this logic, it stands to reason that exploiting the natural world is somehow beneficial. The mantra incessantly repeats it's the economy OR your environment. Living in filth is profitable for you. Trust us. you will have more money to spend on bottled water, air purifiers, antibiotics for infections resulting from contaminated water, and better health insurance coverage.

Ask yourself, why is fossil fuel extraction through fracking and wastewater injection into aquifers permitted and even encouraged when it poisons drinking water supplies in a time when water shortages are critical? Where is the discussion on other technologies such as cold fusion, which essentially fuses hydrogen atoms in a low energy nuclear reaction? The result of which is excess heat energy with no toxic emissions, or radioactive waste.

Our legal system makes it perfectly lawful to contaminate water, air, and land—where corporations are granted certain rights by our Constitution to pre-empt local laws regardless of the health and economic consequences for the community. This, however, is slowly changing, as described in the Legal Rights for Ecosystems section. None of these scenarios will really change unless all land, water, and wildlife are regarded as living beings with equal rights to exist. The irony is that the more the natural world flourishes the more human beings prosper, in every sense of the word. Yet we continue to shoot ourselves in the feet.

Mainstream society has it backwards—by design. The current system allows the few to control the many. It has always been about power and control, which results from over-dependence on centralized systems. Go back in history as far as you want and there is a systematic centralization of power, resources, and decision-making. See the section on the U.S. Constitution compared to the original Articles of Confederation. The power structure needs to transform into a **true democratic** society. I am not naïve enough to think it can happen from the top. This will most probably occur from the bottom up, because the controlling elite will relentlessly strive to hold onto their power at all costs, and maintain the current destructive (but profitable to them) status quo. Real estate can be used as a vehicle to change the house rules in favor of life, economic prosperity, self-reliance, and health. **It doesn't have to be one or the other.** It is actually more financially profitable to work with the forces of the natural world than to impose inefficient and destructive systems that may solve one problem while creating three more at greater expense.

Microbiologist Rene Dubos wrote the Pulitzer prize-winning book: So Human an Animal: How We're Shaped by Surroundings and Events. In this book, he explains how humans are becoming more and more dehumanized by the deteriorating condition of our environment and that there is a direct correlation between human health and the condition of our ecosystems. He says:

> Humans can adopt to starless skies, treeless avenues, shapeless buildings, tasteless bread, spiritless pleasures ... it is questionable that man can retain his physical and mental health if he loses contact with the natural forces that have shaped his biological and mental nature.

Why is this? Most probably because everything in the natural world is interconnected on some level. Just because our five senses cannot always pick up on this does not mean the connection isn't there. After all, visible light and audible sound represent only a very tiny fraction of the entire electromagnetic spectrum. Just because we cannot perceive it directly through the five senses does not mean it isn't there. This may partly explain certain feelings one gets walking through old growth forests, subconsciously picking up on the energy there. Ludwig van Beethoven often took long walks through the forests, quite possibly to get inspiration from this energy.

The reasons behind these observations are being researched and documented now more than ever. German forester Peter Wohlleben wrote an excellent book, "The Hidden Life of Trees: What They Feel, How They Communicate – Discoveries from a Secret World." He reveals the vast communication networks between trees—how they emit signals to warn other trees of oncoming problems, and help restore health to other damaged trees. The world is alive, intelligent and interconnected, not an isolated series of random events.

We appear to have a problem seeing a larger, whole-systems approach when viewed through the eyes of narrow specialization and short-term profit. You can start reversing this trend now, literally in your own back yard, using your residential or commercial property to create a new paradigm for profitable cooperation with the natural world rather than a controlling and dominating one.

Real estate investment analyses and operating statements for various types of sustainable upgrades and designs will demonstrate their viability and profitability, or not. Not all sustainable design works economically, and a lot depends on the specific situation. Basic principles can be directly applied or modified to fit the parameters of a given property. Discussing potential problems in an objective, non-biases, inclusive manner paves the way for creative solutions.

Today's precipitous increases in energy price has sparked intense debate and finger pointing as to the causes and potential solutions. Noticeably absent from these discussions is any talk of reducing the near total reliance on HVAC systems in residential and commercial buildings. In the United States, energy consumption for buildings alone represents some 40% of total energy used. On a global scale its about 35%. Designs that incorporate shading, natural ventilation, wind mitigation, natural light ... can significantly reduce this consumption, and take a major step towards energy independence. The public has been conditioned to ignore this and rather focus on more drilling, solar panels, and wind farms, all of which are expensive, wasteful, inefficient and non-renewing in the absolute sense of the word. They all get used up or worn out, and need to be periodically replaced. True renewable designs last forever, get better over time, require little to no maintenance, and are inexpensive. They operate as symbiotic ecosystems that create little to no waste.

The narrative needs to change in favor of these designs. That, however may not happen for awhile as the controlling interests do not want to relinquish their power or influence. Wars over oil are good for business; an independent, self-reliant public is not. They must continue to mold and shape public opinion and perception through a corporate media obediently reciting their talking points.

The term regenerating systems may be a more accurate description as compared to sustainable or green. The principle is about putting back as much as you take from the surrounding area, or as close to it as possible. The late architect Malcolm Wells aptly stated this principle as follows:

> A building should consume its own waste, maintain itself, match nature's pace, provide wildlife habitat, moderate climate and weather and be beautiful. That's a series of pass/fail evaluation criteria. We live in an era of glitzy buildings and trophy houses: big, ugly, show-off monsters that stand—or I should say stomp—on land stripped bare by the construction work and replanted with toxic green lawns. If the buildings could talk they would be speechless with embarrassment, but most of us see nothing wrong with them, and would, given the opportunity, build others like them, for few of us realize that there's a gentler way to build.

Land Planning and New Building Developments

You can attend almost any city council meeting and discover one common theme: lack of funds for important infrastructure projects. Why is this? One reason is adhering to failing development models. Bringing new shiny buildings to the outskirts of town makes any city official look good, and has the illusion of progress and more tax revenue. The truth is, if more emphasis was placed on sustainably renovating and/or redesigning older structures closer to downtown, the tax revenue per acre would be many times that of outlying areas, and without the extra needed infrastructure such as sewers, electrical lines, water hook-ups, roads, etc.. In addition, the land required for this new development would remain untouched, in its pristine state, for people and animals to enjoy.

Again, there are many variables to take into account when quantifying the benefits of a given project. All too often, decisions are based on antiquated, overly simplistic development models that have the most splash. If the politicians were truly interested in making their towns more solvent, they should take the time to evaluate alternative options laid out in this book. More on this will be covered in the Land Planning chapter.

The cities of Basel, Lucerne, and Zurich Switzerland now require all new flat roofs to be green, vegetated rooftops. Why is America behind? As mentioned, the status quo is profitable for some people and they like things just as they are. The media is another issue. The American mainstream media has, for the most part, turned a blind eye to the financial, economic, and environmental benefits of regenerating principles. Why? Maybe because if it isn't high tech, it isn't worth mentioning, or, because they are entrenched in the old paradigm of the environment vs. the economy. They hold firm the belief that environmental degradation and pollution is a natural side effect of "progress." These hidden costs are not factored into corporate balance sheets, while everyone else pays in the form of higher taxes and disease. It is a profitable business model for the offenders, thus it is perpetuated to this day.

Information Molds Perception

I have conducted numerous interviews with architects and land planners on the subjects of, building performance, land use, and development. Our discussions examined new designs, materials, and construction methods that make buildings more efficient, durable, and resilient in the face of severe weather. At the conclusion of these interviews, one question invariable arose. That is, if all we have discussed carries with it so many benefits in terms of property values, cost reduction, environmental/physical health and overall wellbeing, why aren't they used in mainstream building and development? The response was that builders are very slow to change and are looking for the quickest paycheck from their developments—in and out, then on to the next project. They don't want to be bothered learning new methods when the status quo has served them relatively well for so many years. Many architects also agree that most builders are behind the times in implementing new designs, materials and methodologies.

Another reason for this slow response is the perceived lack of data that substantiates all the benefits of more symbiotic designs. There are numerous well-documented case studies that present detailed, quantifiable results on the financial, health, and environmental benefits. The problem is that much of this information is not readily available through centralized sources; nor is it and broken down into easily discernable facts on which to base decisions.

Perception is molded by information received, The mainstream media repeatedly bombards us with lies and misinformation about accepting, as progress, the toxic cesspool we now live in. It's a price we must pay to live in a modern society, they say. Viable alternatives are rarely discussed or taken seriously, unless of course there is a lot of money to be made on new patented technology, biotechnology, etc. And those will seemingly solve one problem (Although it is usually just a temporary fix.) while creating two others. And, as if builders were not slow enough, government bureaucracies are even slower in response to desperately needed changes.

This book is the culmination of countless interviews and extensive research to in order to put this information into the hands of people who will implement it now, and receive all the benefits from doing so. This will most likely be happening from the likes of individual property owners, managers, tenants, etc. who want to change the direction from waste and pollution to regeneration and profit.

Perceptions Manifest as Reality

Before going on to the financial analyses and benefits, it is appropriate to look back to the original stewards of this land, the Native Americans. We can/should learn from their true democratic governments, where special interests could not exist in their participatory democracies, where respect for the land, air, water, and all living things were part of their everyday life. These are the people that helped form our government, as many concepts from the original Iroquois Confederacy were adopted into our constitution

Respecting the land was not only a Native American concept; it was also deeply rooted in the minds of some founding fathers. According to Thomas Jefferson, the earth belongs to the living.

> No man can by natural right oblige the lands he occupied, or the persons who succeeded him in that occupation, to the payment of debts contracted by him. For if he could, he might during his own life eat up the usufruct of the lands for several generations to come, and then the lands would belong to the dead, and not the living.

It is in my opinion that in order for true sustainability to hit the mainstream, we should take a deep look at the priorities of our society and government, and learn from history, beginning with the indigenous people of the United States. Most probably the biggest rift between Western society and Native Americans lies in differing fundamental belief systems about the nature of reality. Indigenous cultures feel spiritually connected to every aspect of the world—mountains, streams, plains, animals—which they believed to be alive and interconnected with all else. Industrialized society views everything in the world as separate, and available for exploitation. You can read more on this in the Indigenous Wisdom chapter which goes to the root of today's environmental problems.

Economic gain should not come at the expense of the natural world. On the contrary, management and development that emphasizes the integration and regeneration of natural systems is more profitable in every sense of the word.

If you are comfortable with the status quo, and believe your best interests are being served, then it is probably not necessary, or beneficial for you to read on. However, if you feel there is a better way to manage land, ecosystems and buildings, and are willing to incorporate some of these methods into your own property, then please read on. While reading, keep an open mind as to how these principles can be best applied to your unique situation.

At the next planning board meeting in your area, offer concrete solutions to the problems at hand, and begin a discussion on the opportunities and benefits to be gained from making certain changes. It is usually a win-win scenario for all involved. However, you will probably come across board members and/or local politicians whose minds are so rigid and programmed that no matter what irrefutable evidence you present their answers will always be the same. They may seem to have lost the ability to think critically and objectively analyze the facts before them. Their belief systems dictate the way in which they perceive the world. Anything outside their little perceptual bubbles, in their minds is just not worthy of discussion. This general milieu has never been more evident than now, in 2023, the age of identity politics, ideological division, and group think.

Chapter Three

Indigenous Wisdom

How true democracy really functioned—for all life

Everything connects to everything else.
– Leonardo da Vinci

Society is becoming more and more dependent on technology, in every facet of life. This technology is promised to create a more comfortable, secure, and productive lifestyle, while saving the planet from environmental devastation. Man seems hell-bent on solving, with his own technology, the very problems he created. That usually means imposing his will on the natural world rather than working with it—an ego-centric sense of superiority and entitlement which may solve one problem, but usually creates two more in the process.

Solving problems that create permanent and positive change, with no collateral damage may require a deeper look into the underlying belief systems of modern society's relation to the natural world. Indigenous cultures and the industrialized world have drastically different perceptions of this. Native Americans (the Plains Indians in particular) perceive time, place and the world as cyclical—the seasons, night and day, birth-death, ecosystem regeneration, etc. These cycles are in a perpetual state of movement and transformation, which is inherent in the rhythm of nature. At the middle of these cycles is a constant, changeless, and timeless center, referred to as the great mystery, the indwelling presence, the Great Spirit, or God.

These cycles and rhythms are found everywhere in the natural world, and as such, all nature is considered sacred and interrelated, including Native Americans themselves. To desecrate a lake or a mountain would be analogous to harming one's own body, since nature is an extension of their own being.

According to the late Tonya Gonnella Frichner, of the Onondaga Nation:

> How can you "save the earth" if you have no spiritual relationship with the earth? There is an intellectual abstraction about the environment, but no visceral participation with the earth. Non-Indians cannot change the current course of destruction without this connection.

Tonya was a lawyer and professor of American Indian history. She worked in the New York City metropolitan area to advance indigenous rights and promote understanding between all cultures. Her work brought her in contact with many tribes across the nation. Each was unique in some ways, but one underlying principle remained constant, that the Native Americans' relationship to the earth was "identical" across all tribes.

Land viewed as spiritual, alive and interrelated creates a mutual respect. Anita Barrows in Biophilia Hypothesis wrote:

> It is only by a construct of the Western mind that we believe ourselves to be living in an "inside" bounded by our own skin, with everything and everyone else on the outside. The place where transitional phenomena occur ... might be understood in this new paradigm of the self, to be the permeable membrane that suggests or delineates, but does not divide us from the medium in which we exist.

That is to say, we are more than our physical bodies. Our energy fields extend far beyond the skin and interact with other fields. There is a connection on this wavefield/energetic level which many indigenous cultures feel as expanded awareness.

A cross within a circle symbolized the Plains Indians' relationship with nature. The cross unites the four corners of the universe with the vertical axis connecting the sky and earth. At the center of the axis are human beings, central to and connected with all of nature. The indwelling presence or Great Spirit is within human beings and within everything else in the natural world; therefore, Native Americans feel they are connected with nature on a much deeper, sacred level.

Joseph Brown, in his book The Spiritual Legacy of the American Indian, quoted Black Elk, an elder member of the Sioux nation:

> Peace ... comes within the souls of men when they realize their relationship, their oneness with the universe and all its powers, and when they realize that at the center of the Universe dwells Wakan-Tanka, and that this center is really everywhere, it is within each of us.

He goes on to say that human beings are not only part of nature, but also have a divine purpose to protect, watch over and work with nature. This is a concept shared among most indigenous cultures where all supposed inanimate objects are really alive and interconnected to all life. The world is not there for them to exploit, but is seen as equal to, and one of them.

Modern society's relationship with the natural world is almost opposite to the Native American's sense of spiritual connectedness. The definition of a human being in Webster's dictionary is: *man in his distinctive facilities, capacities, or spheres of action as contrasted with the rest of nature, with the animal, or with the divine.* Therein lies one important distinction with indigenous cultures—**human beings contrasted with the rest of nature**—and most probably goes to the source of many environmental disasters we face today.

Another difference is the perception of time. Native Americans also view time as cyclical, as opposed to Western man's linear sense of time—a straight line with no beginning, end point, or center. Cyclical time revolves around a changeless center, which gives meaning to time.

Linear time, without the true center of changeless permanence, goes on and on into an uncertain and indefinite future. Can change have meaning and purpose if not relative to a changeless center? This may in part explain today's treadmill mentality, of franticly running toward an illusionary future point, producing more and more goods and technology to feed a ravenous consumer population programmed to think bigger. Thus, more is not only better, but necessary to maintain our "high standard of living." The by-product is systematic destruction of living systems and the wanton extraction of resources using the fastest and cheapest means possible. Native Americans' relation to their changeless center within themselves and the natural world gives them meaning and purpose, irrespective of the Dow Jones or the Gross National Product.

This concept of selfless, inseparable unity with nature is not just a Native American belief. The West has also accepted it. Jill Bolte Taylor, a Harvard-trained brain scientist (neuroanatomist) suffered from a hemorrhage in the left side of her brain. This cut off much of the blood flow to this region of the brain, and essentially closed it down. Left brain functions include analytical, linguistic, and calculating skills. This rendered her unable to speak, comprehend language, or perform any type of linear processing. The left brain is also responsible for the constant chatter we hear in our minds, and the sense of our physical selves being alone and separate from all else.

Her right brain functioned normally. This hemisphere does not discern borders or limitations, but rather sees unity and connection with all things. It reveals a bigger picture of how everything relates with no boundaries, compartmentalization, or hierarchical structure.

It is peaceful, quiet, and constantly in the present, with no sense of time. She writes in her book, *A Stroke of Insight,* that she felt the power of a life force universal energy and could not delineate where her body ended, as it seemed to merge seamlessly with the energy fields around her.

Anger, hatred, greed, fear, etc., are left brain functions emanating from its perception of people being fragile, limited individuals living in isolation. She believes the right brain should not be neglected in favor of the analytical, busy-body left brain, as it is, for the most part, in today's society. We should be striving for more balance between the two, and listening with open minds to the wisdom of Indigenous culture.

I believe the real starting point of sustainability is not the latest gadgets of technology, but rather your belief systems and spirituality. If the natural world is not regarded as sacred, with a spiritual connection to man, then all attempts at a sustainable world are random, temporary, and with no solid foundation.

Spirituality was/is part of the economic and political life of Native Americans. It could be seen as a great system of checks and balances. If economic prosperity were to be acquired at the expense of spirituality (which also held the land as sacred) it would not be permitted. Only when spirituality was in accord with economics and politics would any final decision be made. This eliminated short-term gain at the expense of long-term prosperity. The business model of the West seems to be ever more fixated on short-term profits regardless of long-term consequences. We see these long term consequences surfacing in all corners of the planet.

According to Carolyn Merchant, professor at the University of California at Berkeley and author of The Death of Nature:

> The earth was regarded as a living creature until the scientific revolution of the 1700s. The earth was held in this regard by Western civilizations as well as indigenous cultures. The soil,

> the air, the water, the plants and animals were all part of one living being. The treatment of the earth reflected this philosophy until the onslaught of science in the 1700s.

This "Age of Enlightenment" viewed the earth as dead, while putting man above and separate from it with a sense of entitlement (conquer/exploit nature) to do whatever he wished.

This sense of the world was completely at odds with Native American culture, and as such, made it virtually impossible for the two to co-exist. It is no wonder many, if not most Indian tribes do not want to assimilate into modern society. They may see it as a path to inevitable destruction, which they want no part of. Many see themselves as eventually inheriting their sacred land once again. Right now, there is a huge void between the two cultures, and conventional wisdom would have us believe they are mutually exclusive and incompatible by definition.

Living in unity may sound impossible, but only in the old mindset of limitation—the economy or the environment, me or you. It sounds impossible because the proponents of the divisive status quo will not even bring indigenous values into the discussion. They are labeled extinct, primitive, and backward. This is one way to deny their value or outright existence. When the discussion rises above limiting belief systems (imposed by the elite, special interest groups controlling the media, finance, governments...), to the level of cooperation, respect, and expanded awareness, the benefits for all living beings are limitless.

We are a society dominated by analytical, calculating, structured thinking. Playing not to lose is not good enough. The juggernaut of corporate greed has placated the population into accepting disease, resource depletion, and toxic waste as "necessary and normal." Incorporating a whole new set of rules is what is needed. Why cover-up symptoms of a problem when you can create a paradigm that, by its very nature, never allows the problem to surface in the first place?

Why isn't this even being brought up in the debates? Through mind-numbing repetition the mainstream media has instilled the mantra of necessary "collateral damage," which includes filthy air, water, and the resulting diseases into the minds of "consumers" who should be thankful that they have electricity at all. Dirty air and disease is a small price to pay for such a "high" standard of living, right? Cancer is a necessary and inevitable by-product of progress, right?

Better stated, cancer is a by-product of a negligent businesses not being held accountable for the toxic waste they release into the air and water.. The reason this continues is that many people buy into the line that it is too expensive to fix or that there is no better way.

Do we as human beings really think it is necessary to live and work in our own waste? Are we that stupid? No, certainly not. But if you repeat a lie enough times, it will eventually be perceived as truth. Members of Adolph Hitler's Reich Ministry of Propaganda and Enlightenment led by Joseph Goebbels, were masters at this.

If it were really too expensive, then a prudent CEO would bring in a new management team to creatively eliminate this expensive problem and turn it into a positive cash-flow solution. Impossible? Is this delusional dreaming? The problem here is that a business model that profits from sustainability, regeneration, co-existence, and health is not even discussed in the mainstream. It seems to be a foregone conclusion that filth, disease, and poverty HAVE to be part of the equation.

You can create your **own** business model. Real estate solutions are outlined in the following pages, backed by numbers that don't lie. Now is the time to break down the illusory walls of limitation, scarcity, and fear in favor of a more right-brained, larger picture, creative approach.

Many problems would never even come into existence if the larger governing structures worked primarily in the best interests of all living beings. This would be more in line with the Iroquois Confederacy than English Common Law, which was structured to expand the

British Empire.

Native American culture is relevant in this discussion because modern society has learned a lot more from their culture and ways of governance than the history books would have us believe, and there is a lot more we can learn and apply today. The problems created by modern-day energy/water/land use policies go beyond technology and need to be addressed at the source.

There is a larger picture of true democracy in action that would not allow for the global destruction that is rampant today. The greed of the controlling elite would not be tolerated by the many. This is where we can, and should, finally recognize the wisdom of Native American culture and their truly democratic forms of government.

The Four Commandments of Native Americans are:

1) respect for Mother Earth
2) respect for the Great Spirit
3) respect for fellow man and woman
4) respect for individual freedom

Today, our individual freedoms are under attack like never before, such as the right to free speech, and the right to bear arms. The earth is being ravaged by, among other things, building development and management models that value the bulldozer over regenerating, life-supporting natural systems. The picture looks rather bleak when you add to that supply chain disruptions, runaway inflation, and food scarcity. It is blatantly obvious government bureaucracies don't have your back. They are more interested in never ending wars. That said, your best option may be to become more self-reliant and independent, and in so doing help create a new paradigm of prosperity, health and abundance.

Why reinvent the wheel when Native Americans can teach us how to protect this earth, treat it as a living being, and save it from a slow death, just as they taught the original thirteen colonies how to survive in North America. These underlying principles combined with regenerating architecture and land/water management could transform modern society.

Not only did Native Americans teach the colonies survival skills, but their governing principles helped form the original Articles of Confederation, and to a lesser extent, the United States Constitution. Many of our founding fathers recognized the wisdom behind Native American government and consulted with them, particularly the Iroquois.

George Clinton, governor of New York from 1777 to 1795, spoke about the shortcomings of American democratic leaders as, *"People of republican principles who have no knowledge of democratic governments."* James Madison studied and spoke with Iroquois leaders on a regular basis. Thomas Jefferson often referred to their governing structure in his writings. According to UC Berkeley Professor Donald Grinde, Benjamin Franklin brought his colleagues together to "hammer out a plan" that he acknowledged to be similar to the Iroquois Confederacy.

When expressing his desire to evolve from the European form of government and incorporate more Native American principles, Franklin wrote:

> The care and labor of providing for artificial and fashionable wants, the sight of so many rich wallowing in superfluous plenty, while so many are kept poor and distressed for want; the insolence of office ... and restraints of custom all contrive to disgust them [Indians] with what we call civil society.

While trying to rally support from the colonies, and formulate a freer, more democratic system of government, Franklin cited basic principles of the Iroquois Confederacy:

> All the Indians of North America not under the dominion of the Spaniards are in that natural state, being restrained by no laws, having no courts, or Ministers of Justice, no suits, no pris-

> ons, no governors vested with any legal authority. The persuasion of men distinguished by reputation of wisdom is the only means by which others are governed, or rather led—and the state of the Indians was probably the first State of all Nations.

There was and continues to be outright denial that the original American government had anything to do with the Iroquois "savages." However, as more people tend to mistrust our own political system, as evidenced by poor voter turnout, there may be renewed interest in the Iroquois Confederacy, specifically its influences on our original Constitution, and how far we have strayed from its true intent.

There are many features of the Iroquois Confederacy found within the U.S. Constitution, such as a system of checks and balances, representation at the state and federal level, separate powers for the states, and resources for the defense of the nation. There are also some not used in our Constitution:

1) The chiefs had no absolute executive power (even for war), with all policy determined by consensus at every level of government.
2) Women were given the power to remove chiefs if they were not performing properly.
3) All natural resources could not be owned, bought, or sold.

One primary distinction, which helped facilitate consensus by all the people, was the participation of Pine Tree Chiefs. These were common people who demonstrated knowledge of current affairs and proved trustworthy and wise. They were given the opportunity to participate in all discussions at every level of the Confederacy. Imagine if that were the case today. Any citizen of this character could participate in congressional debates, energy policy meetings, and war planning rooms. Everything would be out in the open for all to hear and see. Special interest lobbyists and politicians could no longer conceal their agendas.

The Confederacy had certain guiding principles. Paragraph 12 of the Iroquois Constitution states:

> The thickness of their skin shall be seven spans, which is to say they block out anger, offensive actions, and criticisms. Their hearts shall be full of peace and good will and their minds filled with a yearning for the welfare of the people of the Confederacy. With endless patience, they shall carry out their duty and their firmness shall be tempered with a tenderness for their people. Neither anger nor fury shall find lodgment in their minds and all their words and actions shall be marked by calm deliberation ... must be honest in all things.... Self-interest must be cast out into oblivion ... look and listen for the welfare of the whole people and have always in view not only the present but the upcoming generations, even for those whose faces are yet beneath the surface of the ground and unborn of the future Nation.

Another aspect of the Great Law of the Iroquois Confederacy is that any major decision literally goes back to the people for a consensus. In order to assure the will of the people is duly represented, the council is not authorized to make any decisions without this. When was the last time the American people were consulted on health care, pre-emptive war, energy policies, agriculture, or anything else with major ramifications?

What if these principles were used in developing the energy policy of the United States? Do you really think the people would agree to give more taxpayer money in the form of subsidies to support energy companies that emit toxic chemicals into the water and air? Again, the belief is that there is no better way. You have to live with the filth and disease or pay more for your energy. There are better ways. Industrial scrubbers effectively remove toxic gasses such as Mercury, Nitrous Oxide and Sulphur Dioxide from power plants and other industrial polluters. Why aren't they used on a larger scale, and why are better, more efficient prototypes not being developed?

The mainstream media is silent on this.

Hydraulic fracking is a widespread means of extracting oil and gas from shale, limestone, and sandstone, etc. using high pressure water streams to fracture rock formations, allowing oil and/or gas to escape. The by product is highly contaminated water that is typically piped back down into underwater aquifers. There are solutions, such as portable water treatment systems that could effectively clean up the contaminated water, on site. See the Water Management chapter for more on this. The offending energy companies need to pony up the money required to implement these and other measures. After all, we the people are subsidizing them, and one would think that is the least they could do.

What do you think the elected leaders, Pine Tree chiefs, and people of the Iriquois Confereracy would say? The consensus would be anything that desecrates ecosystems on which all life depends must stop immediately, or modified to enhance these systems rather than destroy them.

According to a New York Times/CBS poll, 79% of the people believe that big interests looking out for themselves run the government. When asked about a 3rd political party, the most frequent answer was to have one which truly "represents the people." This is not about complaining, but rather seeing things for what they are and replacing an old, fixed set of rules with a new paradigm devoid of deception or greed. Creative management is used here as a microcosm, a blueprint if you will, for this new paradigm.

This is a way to create a new self-sustaining democracy, a system that will work for generations to come, not a short-term, profit grabbing, self-destructive policy. It is also a way to get it done now, from the ground up, without waiting and hoping for an "enlightened" government to all of a sudden show up.

These changes are already occurring. Films are being produced from Native American perspectives, and reveal their empathy and spirituality as opposed to the classic Hollywood screaming savage running in circles around a stagecoach. As Claudia Gorbman writes in her book *Western Music and Its Others*, the Indian was portrayed as an "obstacle to the fulfillment of manifest destiny" in pre World War II western films:

> It pits the meaningless, bureaucratic, greedy, wasteful, stupid culture of the U.S. Army against the unified culture, generosity, intelligence, gentle humor, and respect for the earth that characterize the Sioux.

Gorbman goes on to say western films later depicted Geronimo as a symbol of what America has lost—"vitality, purity of spirit, community, commitment." The wild west was/is also portrayed as succumbing to a reality of technological advancement and capitalistic exploitation at the expense of the land and its people, while lamenting the loss.

As mentioned earlier, Thomas Jefferson, James Madison, and Thomas Paine, among others studied and spoke with Iroquois leaders on a regular basis to learn more about their strong and purely democratic government. Caldwallader Colden held many offices within the colonies, including lieutenant governor of New York. He also studied anthropology and other natural sciences, which helped shape his political views. He was particularly interested in the Iroquois government, as it revealed the flaws and antiquity of their own European government. He wrote about the Iroquois leaders whose authority and power was given to them by the people and based primarily on their wisdom and integrity. There was no place for political maneuvering or power plays, and once elected, they never imposed their will upon the people by compulsion or force.

The native society's government by "natural law" helped bring about the revolution in America. Franklin, Jefferson, and Paine strove to bring as much of that law as they could into their own democracy. The question that remained was how did these indigenous people, who valued personal liberty above all else, retain any form of social unity and adherence to law. James Adair wrote in his book *History of the American Indians:*

> The Indian method of government ... in general ... consists of a federal union for mutual safety. The Indians, therefore, have no such titles, or persons as emperors, or kings, or an appellative for such, in any of their dialects.... They have no words to express despotic power, arbitrary kings, oppressed, or obedient subjects.... The power of their chiefs is an empty sound. They can only persuade or dissuade the people, either by the force of good nature and clear reasoning, or by coloring things, so as to suit the prevailing passions. It is reputed merit alone that gives them any titles or distinctions.

The Native American political philosophy was that all life was spiritually unified with the natural environment. They did not respect submissive people who cowered under authority, as the children were all taught to think for themselves in a way that upheld individual freedoms. (Compare that with the group think and fear mongering of today.) This all added to shaping the American Revolution. British philosopher John Locke wrote of governments that were grounded in this natural state and without absolute executive power, similar to the Great Law of the Iroquois Confederacy. Locke went on to agree with most aspects of the Iroquois Confederacy except for the concept of private property. This concept of ownership was so deeply entrenched in the social and political system that it had to be retained, although Thomas Jefferson tried to substitute the concept of happiness for property ownership.

There continued to be disputes, not about Indigenous governments, but about just how much of it to include in their own new government. Thomas Jefferson said that force and corruption were the mainstays of every modern government and went on to argue that there is nothing more ridiculous than killing in the name of peace and love. Samuel Adams was primarily interested in defeating the

English and adopting minor changes in the new government, while Franklin wished to completely destroy the old government.

On June 6, 1776, the Iroquois chiefs were invited to the hall of the Continental Congress to help draw up a Declaration of Independence that would embrace the same rights as the "natural societies of the native people." Franklin and Jefferson both wanted as much consensus of the people as possible and to retain other laws similar to the Iroquois political structure. Local problems were solved locally, larger problems solved by a national government, and with weak executive powers. We have strong executive powers today and little consensus of the people, as most policies are drawn up behind closed doors.

Robert Reich, Professor of Public Policy at the University of California, Berkeley, and author of *Supercapitalism: The Transformation of Business, Democracy, and Everyday Life*, had some comments about capitalism, politics, and democracy:

> I think it better to acknowledge the natural desire of human beings to improve their material conditions, but to understand how easily today's consumers seeking great deals in this hyper -competitive economy inadvertently trump their concerns as citizens who value the common good.

According to Mr. Reich, politics should create more distance from the capitalist business system, insuring no undue influence by special interests and specific industries, and with citizens taking a more proactive role in the political system. The result would be similar to Indigenous democratic systems. The only difference being, in the case of Native Americans, government and spirituality were intertwined, with no need for separation.

Symbolism in Nature

Symbols represent that which is not so easily described with words. They embody ideas, beliefs, and experiences in a vivid and

Figure 1a The Eastern White Pine–a symbol of peace, unity, and security in the Iroquois Confederacy and beyond

powerful manner that words cannot equal. The complexities and interrelationships of all life run too deep for scientific terms and explanations alone. Since Native Americans have such a deep, spiritual connection with the land, aspects of the natural world are used to symbolize and bring to light the inexplicable.

The eastern white pine represents the unification of Indian nations in peaceful coexistence, and the merging of human and spiritual law with the laws of nature. The four white roots extend North, South, East and West connecting the nations of the confederacy and beyond, while guiding them to the peace, security and shelter of the towering white pine branches.

Prior to the formation of the Iroquois Confederacy, the Cayuga, Oneida, Seneca, Onondaga, and Mohawk engaged in bloody feuds and wars. According to legend, a "peacemaker" travelled from the shores of Lake Huron to visit the five nations with a message of peace and unity. He used the white pine Tree of Peace to symbolize that message. This constant reminder of the peacemaker's wisdom helped manifest the Iroquois League of Nations.

The Big Picture

In the preceding pages many references were made to Native American government structure, spirituality, and relationship to the land. This was to illustrate the larger picture, where outer actions are a reflection of inner belief systems and values—a mindset that by default produced a sustainable, life-enhancing reality.

It should be repeated that the main function of this book is not to reveal faults in our socio-economic system and point fingers, but rather to help understand these principles in order to manifest a reality geared more towards life, regeneration, health, freedom and profit.

Chapter Four

Dynamic Land Management

Resilient, Problem-Solving Landscapes

We know more about the movement
of celestial bodies than about the soil underfoot.
– Leonardo da Vinci

Sustainable, or regenerating land management is synonymous with efficiency and maximizing all the resources at hand, while reducing costs (both financial and environmental) and profiting from the synergy of natural systems with the built environment. The natural world has an innate ability to solve problems, when given the chance.

Any good management team utilizes **all** available assets for a project. This entails viewing the natural world as a living, integrated being, an intelligent partner that helps maximize efficiency, performance, and profit. To fully reap these benefits, a broad-based knowledge of biological systems, weather patterns, and their cause-effect relationships with the built environment would be in order.

Rather than take the time to fully understand the complex ecosystems of a given area, which would reveal a host of problem-solving, cost-cutting options, many managers look for the fastest most direct means to an end, with little or no thought given to utilizing the landscape and building in a more symbiotic way.

In this digital, information age, society is obsessed with speed where 10 second sound bytes are considered excessive. Speed should not come at the expense of efficiency and the wisdom of the surrounding land. Thomas Jefferson and James Madison talked about information, knowledge and wisdom when framing the Constitution of the United States. They knew information and knowledge were not the same and neither was to be confused with wisdom.

Information and knowledge is a left brain, memorizing function. Wisdom is looking deep down and seeing what is already there, what you already know but are not consciously aware of. It is a right brain, creative, intuitive function that makes the connection between human beings and their surroundings—from isolation to integration and cooperation, from playing solo to performing with the symphony.

In our fast-paced, speed-oriented society, the general consensus appears to be that it's not worth the time and effort to learn and apply regenerating principles to real estate when there are so many "quick fixes" on the market. One needs to re-think this if self-reliance and independence, financial or otherwise, are important.

What is your relationship with the land? Is the land something to be controlled for short-term profit or worked with to get maximum benefit? Is the earth to be used/abused as a machine for material wealth or treated as a living being inseparable from ourselves? This is the Native American philosophy alluded to earlier. Anthropologist Richard Nelson states, "the physical environment is spiritual, conscious, and subject to rules of respectful behavior."

If we continue to forcefully impose our shortsighted will upon the land, with blatant disregard for its problem-solving, life-enhancing forces, the degradation of life and life-supporting systems should come as no surprise. If you wish to become more aligned with Native American wisdom and sustainable philosophies, you can begin by incorporating them into the land/water around you, right now.

The natural world has a direct effect on our health and overall quality of life. According to biologist Hugh Iltis, a child's capacity to develop is directly related to his/her affiliation with nature. Professor Emeritus Paul Sheppard, in his book Coming Home to the Pleistocene, spoke about the adverse effects of "human congestion" and "ecological destitution" on human intelligence and maturity. It reduces a broad, interrelated experience to a narrowly defined reality of separation and mutually exclusive events.

Harvard biologist E.O. Wilson refers to the term biophilia as *"the urge to affiliate with other forms of life."* The children of the Temiar rainforest in Malaysia can rattle off 200-plus plant and animal species and how they interact and coexist. The mountains, wildlife, streams, and rivers—are an integral part of themselves and vice-versa. They receive inspiration and strength from interaction with their natural environment."

Natural systems often solve problems with less cost and no adverse effects while enhancing the quality of life. Using this approach with your real estate gives a higher return on investment, but requires more comprehensive management—using creative thinking in analyzing ever-changing processes and the interaction/synergy of the various elements.

We've become alienated spectators. Sustainable design brings us back into the game. This, however, requires a thorough knowledge of the "playbook," or the workings of the multi-faceted natural systems at your feet. According to anthropologist Levi Strauss in his book Savage Mind:

> Primitive cultures grasp the whole world in a totality of present and past with all its multiplicity and complexity. Civilized thought attempts to simplify rather than clarify the complexity of the world. It seeks continuity and relativity rather than conceptualizing new schemes, as does savage thought ... the civilized mind attempts to simplify and level the world whereas

> the savage mind is not afraid to become enmeshed in its complexity.

Ecosystems are anything but simple. In order to realize their full benefit, managers should become "enmeshed in their complexity."

Cultural historian Thomas Berry in his book The Great Work refers to industry's narrow and over-simplified approach:

> Chaos represents modern science's consternation with its attempt to "tame" the world: its one-factor approach cannot predict in a world of irreducible variables.... Nature cannot be simplified by looking closer and that isolated components have very little value in understanding or prediction.

The Whole Picture

To use a sports metaphor, many fans spend hours on end analyzing teams and devising game plans to defeat the opponent. This is a similar whole-systems approach, as it takes into account all the variables, including players' abilities, the coaching staff, injuries, key match-ups, weather, playing surface (slippery, fast), and play-off implications. Whole systems management looks at potential synergy in the larger picture, and analyzes variables unique to each property in the same manner. These may include climate and weather patterns, topography, size/type/location of plants and trees, or lack thereof, types and heights of surrounding buildings, drainage issues, elevation, soil type, or little to no soil at all (as in inner city neighborhoods), impervious surface area, sun exposure (direction and hours per day), wildlife, and traffic/industrial noise.

These are all factors to take into consideration. For example, photovoltaic cells in solar panels are **less efficient** in hotter climates. This fact alone could/should affect decision making as low-E windows and/or strategically placed shade trees or louvers could provide a better return on investment and more energy savings per dollar spent in hotter climates. Therefore, rather than investing in enough panels to get 100% energy from solar, a combination of two or three elements might be more feasible. This is just one small example of how a comprehensive approach yields greater results than a tunnel-vision, silver-bullet, one-fix-cures-all method.

The first step in managing a site is to sketch out the whole property, including sloping, high and low spots, soil type, any standing water, irrigation requirements, water drainage, flood prone areas, views, position and types of plants and trees, wildlife, sun orientation, position of the building, etc. What is your objective? If it is to provide the highest rate of return, both financially and environmentally, it is a good idea to analyze your property in detail. This is not overwhelming, and can be a very rewarding experience. All it takes is an open mind and a willingness to understand basic biologic and structural systems.

To follow are some practical, low-cost methods that can help you design a more balanced and integrated building/land ecosystem.

Tree Shading

The simplest solutions are quite often overlooked.. The cooling properties of trees and shading should be strongly considered as a means of cutting air-conditioning and electric expense. Summer air-conditioning costs can be reduced from 25 to 50 percent from properly positioned shade trees alone.

Granted, low-E windows are becoming more and more efficient in their ability to insulate from heat, cold, and glare. But even with these improved windows, shading can substantially lower A/C costs in summer, and heating costs in winter as they mitigate cold north winds.

The cooling effects of shading are best realized when the trees are placed to the west, where the hot summer sun is most intense. Shading to the east also helps, but to a much lesser extent, as the morning sun is not as strong. One study (Simpson and McPherson 1996) simulated the shade patterns of two trees on the west side, and

City	Unshaded Cooling Electrical Use kWh	Shaded Annual Electric Use kWh	% Savings
San Diego	418	206	49
Santa Rosa	881	333	38
Sunnyvale	539	282	52
Burbank	1410	403	29
El Toro	1047	355	34
Red Bluff	2135	548	26

Figure 1. Energy savings from two trees planted on the West side and one on the East side of buildings in six California cities.

one tree on the east side, and quantified the energy savings from these trees compared to unshaded residential buildings in six California cities. The results are itemized in figure 1.

Another study (McPherson), showed shade-related air conditioning energy savings from **one** 24-ft. deciduous tree on the west side of residential buildings across the nation (figure 2).

These savings can be substantially increased if the trees were

City	Annual kWh Saved
Atlanta, GA	**255**
Dallas, TX	**285**
Fresno, CA	**390**
Miami, FL	**400**
Tucson, AZ	**400**
Washington DC	**150**

Figure 2 Energy saved from one deciduous tree planted on the West side of homes throughout the country, as compared to similar homes with no trees.

placed to specifically shade under-insulated areas such as large sliding glass doors or windows. The placement would also be customized to shade those window areas at the hottest time of day during the summer months. The "Positioning Trees for Maximum Benefit" section to follow will take you through these calculations.

The cost vs. energy-saving benefits should be analyzed as thoroughly as, say, solar panel design, roof insulation, or thermal windows. The effectiveness of tree/shrub placement will surprise you. As if that wasn't enough, they require little or no maintenance, and have no physical deterioration or functional obsolescence over the years. On the contrary, they become bigger and more efficient as time goes by. We live in a society obsessed with the latest/greatest manufactured product to solve problems. Madison Avenue doesn't advertise trees in TV commercials because there is no profit in it for them, and no proprietary patents to exploit. **You** can profit by implementing tree shading in your business plan if you take the time to study proper placement and sun orientation for your location.

Positioning Trees for Maximum Benefit

The first thing to consider is the section of the structure you want shaded and at what times during the day. In Florida, for example, the high summer sun is more intense on the east and west-facing walls. If this is for cooling purposes, west-facing windows should be the first priority, as the afternoon sun is the strongest in the summer months, with temperatures peaking between 3 and 5 PM. The air conditioning compressor/condenser unit should be considered as well since it will perform more efficiently if cooled by shade.

Let's assume you have a large 12-foot-wide sliding glass door facing west. and would like to block the direct afternoon sun from hitting the glass during the hottest hours of the day. This is accomplished by determining the length and direction of the tree shadows in order to accurately position the trees. The shadows are calculated from the sun's azimuth angle and altitude for a specific location. The

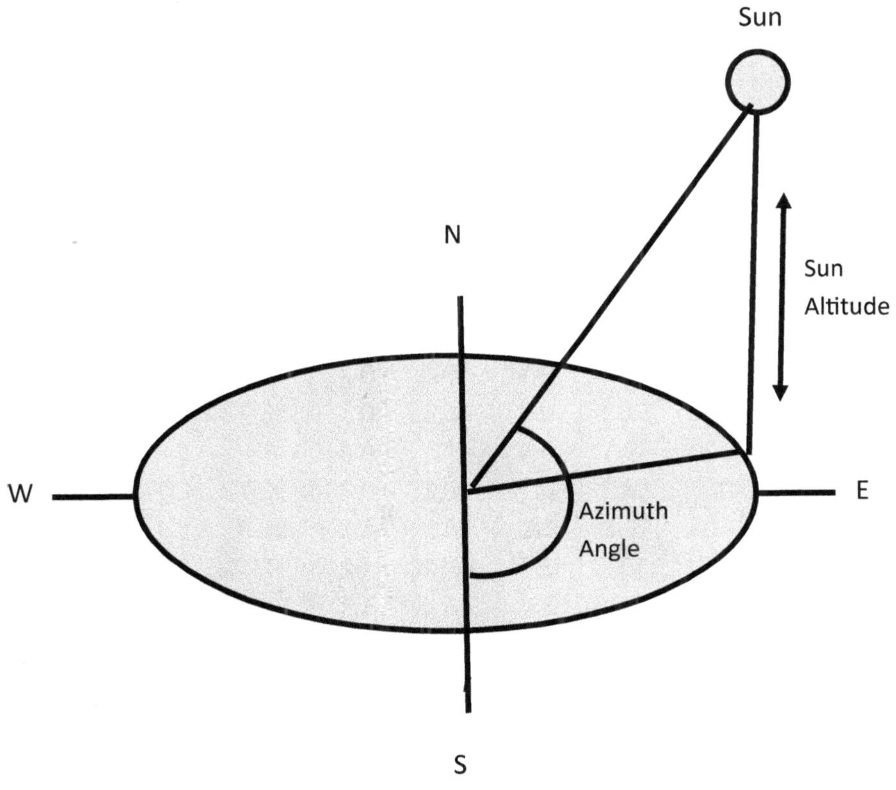

Figure 3 Azimuth angle and sun altitude

sun's altitude is its angle above the horizon, achieving its maximum at solar noon. The azimuth, or bearing angle, is the angle of the sun east or west of true south. See figure 3.

Length and angles of shade can be obtained by using shade-projection charts for specific locations. See figure 4. These indicate the azimuth angles and variables called shade projection factors for given times and locations. The azimuth plots the angle of tree placement relative to the center of the glass door, while the shade projection is part of a formula which determines the distance from the window a tree should be planted.

The first step is to draw a sketch of the building with all win-

Figure 4

Shade Projection Charts Tampa, FL

SPF- Shade Projection Factor

EDT- Eastern Daylight Time; AZ- Azimuth Angle

	JUNE 1		JUNE 8		JUNE 15		JUNE 22	
EDT	SPF	AZ	SPF	AZ	SPF	AZ	SPF	AZ
8AM	3.3	-106.3	3.3	-107.2	3.3	-107.9	3.3	-108.2
9AM	1.7	-100.6	1.7	-101.6	1.8	-102.3	1.8	-102.6
10AM	1.1	-94.8	1.1	-98	1.1	-96.8	1.1	-97.2
11AM	0.7	.88.2	0.7	-89.7	0.7	-90.8	0.7	-91.2
12PM	0.4	-78	0.4	-80.5	0.4	-82.1	0.4	-82.9
1PM	0.2	-47.7	0.1	-53.1	0.1	-57.2	0.1	-59.5
2PM	0.2	52.3	0.2	55.3	0.1	56.7	0.1	56.1
3PM	0.4	79.1	0.4	81	0.4	82	0.4	82.2
4PM	0.7	88.8	0.7	90.1	0.7	90.7	0.7	90.8
5PM	0.1	95.3	1.1	96.2	1.1	96.8	1.1	96.8
6PM	0.8	101	1.8	101.8	1.7	102.2	1.7	102.3
7PM	0.5	106.8	3.4	107.5	3.3	107.8	3.2	107.8

	SEPT. 1		SEPT. 8		SEPT. 15		SEPT. 22	
EDT	SPF	AZ	SPF	AZ	SPF	AZ	SPF	AZ
8AM	5.4	-94.2	5.8	-91.6	6.2	-88.9	6.8	-86.2
9AM	2.3	-87.2	2.3	-84.4	2.4	-81.5	2.5	-78.6
10AM	1.3	-79.2	1.4	-76	1.4	-72.8	1.5	-69.7
11AM	0.9	-68.6	0.9	-64.9	0.9	-61.2	1	-57.6
12PM	0.6	-52	0.6	-47.6	0.6	-43.5	0.7	-39.6
1PM	0.4	-21.7	0.4	-18.1	0.5	-15.1	0.5	-12.4
2PM	0.4	21.2	0.4	20.5	0.5	19.9	0.5	19.4
3PM	0.5	51.7	0.6	49	0.7	46.6	0.7	44.4
4PM	0.6	68.5	0.9	65.7	1	63.2	1.1	60.7
5PM	1.3	79	1.4	76.6	1.5	74.2	1.6	71.9
6PM	2.3	87.1	2.4	84.9	2.7	82.7	3	80.5
7PM	5.3	94.1	6.3	92	7.9	89.9	10.6	87.8

Figure 4 Shading projection chart for central Florida
Source: Enviroscaping to Conserve Energy: Determining Shade Patterns for Central Florida

dows, existing plants, trees and any thing else that may obstruct the sun. Draw a north-south line through the house. This is done in order to line up the protractor later.

We will be shading the sliding glass door facing west, and want the most shade at the hottest times—between 3 and 5 PM from June 15th through September 15th. Since this particular house is in Tampa, FL, the shade projection chart for that area (figure 4) shows the shade projection factor to be .4 and the azimuth to be 82 degrees at 3 PM.

Place the straight edge of a protractor at the midpoint of the slid-

Figure 5
House with shading angles to cover glass door at hottest times of day and year.

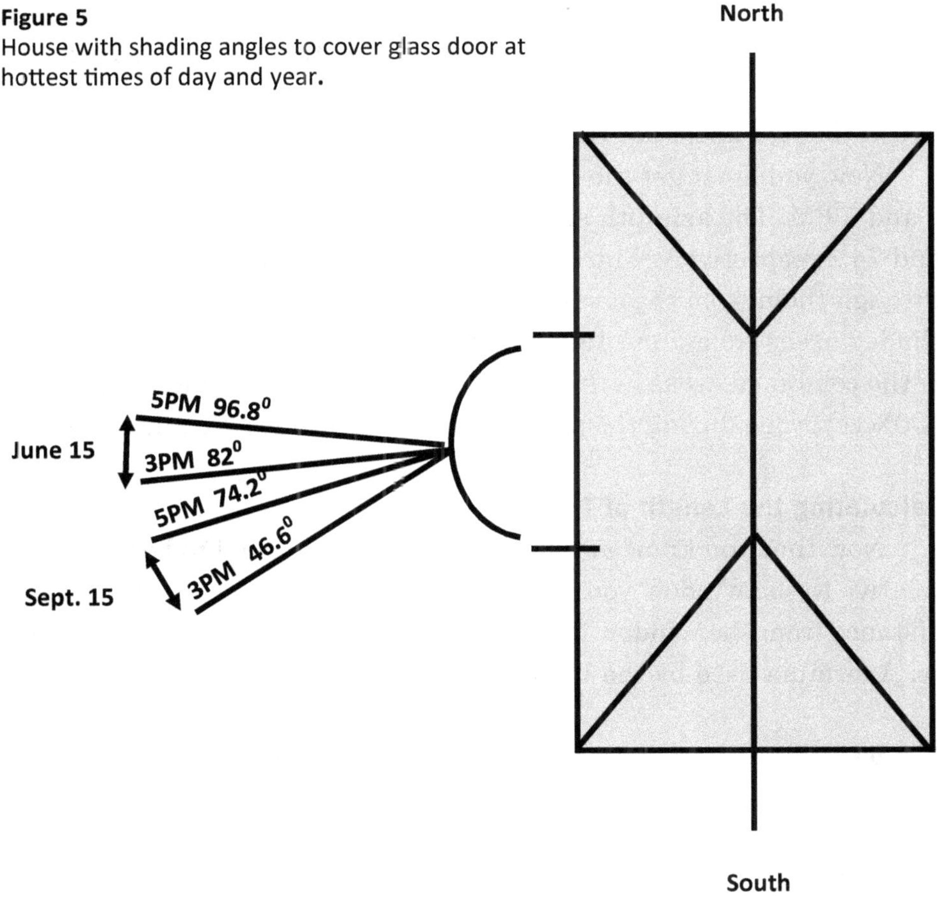

ing glass door with the straight edge facing due south. Here, the straight edge of the protractor should line up parallel to the north-south line you drew.

Start at the southern end of the protractor and move up (northwest) until you hit the azimuth angle on the chart for June 15 at 3 PM, which is 82 degrees. Using the protractor, mark that point on a piece of paper. Next, you have to find the azimuth for 5 PM because we want the most shade to occur between 3 and 5 PM. Mark the azimuth of 96.8 degrees for that time.

Next, draw a line from the midpoint of the sliding glass door to each of the two points just drawn. These lines show the shade angles for June 15th between 3 and 5 PM. To shade the door at 3 PM, a tree must be planted on that line. The same holds true for 5 PM. To get full shade for those times, the tree(s) should cover all the space between the two lines. See figure 5

Now you must get the shade angles for September 15th between 3 and 5 PM. The azimuth angles for 3 and 5 PM on this date are 46.6 and 74.2 respectively. Mark those points on the paper and draw lines through them from the center of the glass door. Now combine the two shaded areas from June 15th to September 15th. The outer two lines of the combined areas is the section that needs to be shaded to get 100% coverage during the specified dates and times. See figure 5.

Calculating the Length of Tree Shadows

Now that you know at what angles the trees need to be planted relative to the window you wish to shade, you need to calculate the distance from the window dependent upon the tree height at maturity. A formula used by the University of Florida is:

X = S (h-h')

S = shade projection factor

h = mature height of the tree in feet

h' = height of the window or anything else you wish to shade

X = the length of the tree's shadow, or the furthest distance from the area to be shaded that the tree should be planted

The sliding glass door is 8' tall. Let us suppose you were to plant a tree that would grow to 30' at maturity. The calculation would be as follows:

The shade projection factor would be .4 on June 15th at 3PM. (See table 4) Therefore: .4 (30-8) = X, or .4(22) = 8.8. The tree should be planted no more than 8.8' from the window for maximum effect along the June 15th angle. The same procedures for June 15th at 5 PM, and September 15th at 3 and 5 PM are:

June 15, 5 PM angle: 1.1 X 22 = 24.2 feet.
June 15, 3 PM angle: .4 X 22 = 8.8 feet
September 15, 5 PM angle: 1.5 X 22 = 33 feet
September 15, 3 PM angle: .7 X 22 = 15.4 feet.

The distances the trees should be planted along these lines are 15'.4', 33', 8.8' and 24.2' respectively.

If, say, you wanted trees no more than 20 feet high, the calculations would change as follows:

June 15, 5 PM angle: 1.1 X 12(20-8) = 13.2 feet.
June 15, 3 PM angle: .4 X 12 = 4.8 feet
September 15, 5 PM angle: 1.5 X 12 = 18 feet
September 15, 3 PM angle: .7 X 12 = 8.4 feet.

More Economics of Shade

Whether you are a believer in global climate change or not, you cannot argue the fact that weather in many areas of the world has become more extreme. This includes the coffee-growing regions of Brazil, Columbia, Costa Rica, Kenya, Ethiopia, and Tanzania. Hotter temperatures adversely affect coffee plants, especially in the higher altitude tropical regions where the plants are more sensitive to slight temperature changes. According to Columbia-based CIAT, (The International Center for Tropical Agriculture) the Tanzanian highlands had a 46% decline in coffee yield over the past 50 years, due to extreme heat. To improve crop production, Arabica coffee crops will have to be moved to cooler areas, some 300-500 meters higher, if they are to thrive in full sun.

The best protection from severe heat is shade. In fact, shade-grown coffee was the primary growing method prior to 1970. It was only after large agribusiness took over the market that bio-diverse areas were bulldozed into large, barren, open fields for intensive mono-crop farming. The logic being that more sun hours made for faster plant growth, producing higher yields and more profit.

Now, due to economic necessity, the cycle has come full circle, as farmers have to resort back to biodiversity and shade in order for sensitive high-altitude coffee crops to survive and thrive.

Roadways

New construction practices today have very little regard for mature trees that provide excellent shading/cooling functions. New street construction usually entails the removal of all trees. To make matters worse, streets have become wider over the years, to accommodate wider street parking areas, and other roadside uses. The loss of shade and the increased asphalt area increases temperatures significantly. On a hot 90-degree day, asphalt temperatures can exceed 140 degrees. This high-surface temperature can increase surrounding air temperature by 10 degrees or more, which translates into additional energy required for cooling surrounding buildings.

Today's race towards more energy efficiency focuses on things like more powerful air conditioners, hermetically sealed building envelopes, and high tech insulation. These are important, but they only reduce symptoms of a problem. One source of the problem—in this case lack of shading and increased asphalt area, is not in the discussion.

It is easier and more efficient to solve virtually any problem, or at least mitigate the effects, by going directly to the source, before the problem has a chance to fully manifest. City planners would do well to consider this when planning a new commercial or residential development or redesigning an old one. Rather than succumb to the almighty bulldozer to level everything in sight, or accept political donations from asphalt companies, they would better serve communities by using all the resources at their disposal, whether it is politically correct or not, whether it is high tech or not.

It is time to get more creative. For example, look at just one advantage of protecting old growth trees. A cafe or restaurant with outdoor seating would benefit tremendously from the shade of an old oak tree. Customers would stay longer in a nicer, cooler environment, and ultimately spend more money. Owners could charge more rent. The local economy would grow as the money trickles down throughout the business community.

There would be no need for business owners to spend money and time placing shades, umbrellas, or fans outside. Their air-conditioning bills would be lower. As added benefits, traffic noise would be somewhat diffused by the foliage, and more stormwater could be absorbed into the ground.

Asphalt area could be reduced by using pervious pavement for on -street parking areas. It would not only reduce the heat island effect, but also would help reduce flooding and filter water back into the underground aquifers, rather than let untreated, dirty water flow into overloaded sewer systems. All this sounds like elementary and overly simplistic common sense, but it is not being done on a any significant level. Most everyone loses except the power, oil, and asphalt companies. This is covered in more detail in the land planning and development chapter.

Tree and Shrub Wind Mitigation

During winter months, strong cold north winds literally suck the heat from buildings. A small grove of trees and shrubs planted on the north side can reduce heating costs by as much as 60 percent, depending on tree height, density, and type.

The Lake States Forest Experimental Station in Nebraska compared two identical test houses. One house was completely exposed to wind, while trees blocked the wind on the other. Both houses maintained a constant indoor temperature of 70 degrees. There was a fuel savings of 22.9% for the wind-protected house.

Another study had a single row of evergreens placed near a building to determine their wind reduction capabilities. Their height was as tall as the building, while the spacing was such that the boughs touched. The distance from the building was between 1.5 and 2 times their height. Many wind velocities were observed and there was an overall reduction of 40% in wind speed. When a fence was placed by the trees, there was a 60% total reduction (Robinette, 1983).

Although a small grove of trees may not block out all of the wind, it can reduce velocity by 50-60%. Another study compared two identical houses—one with trees blocking a 20 mph north wind and the other without tree protection. The wind hitting the protected house was reduced to 5 mph from the trees alone. Heating requirements are significantly reduced as a result.

The most effective wind reduction occurs when the trees are as close to a 90-degree angle to the wind as possible. The coldest winds typically come from the north or northwest (in the northern hemisphere), so it is advisable to orient the trees accordingly.

Sinkholes

According to the United States Geological Survey (USGS), sinkholes are a direct result of inefficient land management—over development, construction practices, and excessive underground pumping. The water chapter explained how sections of California have sunk by 20 feet or more due to inordinate underground water pumping alone.

Given the prevalence of unsustainable building, water, and land use methods, it is no wonder sinkholes are happening more frequently and with greater financial and environmental cost worldwide.

The cause-effect is simple: too much pressure from above and too little resistance from below. Underground pumping combined with little to no aquifer recharging from surface water absorption depletes underground aquifers. This creates a void, empty space the water once occupied. With little support for surface weight, the ground literally sinks down.

The geology of an area plays a role as well. In Florida for example, where sinkholes are an epidemic, much of the underground geology consists of carbonate rock (limestone and dolostone) with varying mixtures of sand and clay on top. Carbonate rock formations store groundwater and have a tendency to slowly dissolve and possibly cave in, causing a sinkhole. This, in addition to excessive weight from buildings, heavy rainfalls, and/or over pumping the underground aquifers, creates the ideal environment for sinkholes.

It should be mandatory for all new construction to absorb as close to 100% of a property's stormwater as possible. This raises the water table, improves drinking water, reduces sinkholes, and prevents flooding. The Water chapter will show how this can be economically and efficiently done with rain gardens, constructed wetlands, biodiversity, and other methods, most of which you can do yourself.

The cost of a sinkhole can be financially devastating to property owners. Just try selling a sinkhole, or sinkhole-repaired property. The sinkhole stigma remains with it—repaired or not. If you get 50-75 cents on the dollar, consider yourself lucky.

Unsustainable building and land use prevails to this day, and at an astronomical economic cost to most. Solutions are relatively simple, but for the most part, it is still business as usual. When major problems occur as a result, everyone acts surprised, and the race is on for new technology to save the day. If you want to know why things do not really change on a mainstream level, just follow the money. Whose pockets are being lined from conventional solutions to problems—problems that should not have happened in the first place?

Toxic Soil Cleanup Using Mushrooms

Land contamination from garbage dump-sites, industry, chemical dumping, etc., often goes unnoticed until adverse health effects become evident. There are thousands of toxic waste sites in the U.S. earmarked for clean-up by the EPA. There are thousands more smaller sites that are not even reported. Although not as obvious as air and water pollution, land contamination is just as hazardous. The government is overloaded and cannot come close to cleaning them all up, even with their super funds earmarked especially for these types of sites. The onus falls squarely upon individuals to clean up any contaminated soil within their property borders and beyond. One of the most efficient and least expensive means in which to do this is with the strategic placement and cultivation of mycelium-rich mushrooms. Mycelium within the mushroom excretes enormous quantities of enzymes, anti-microbial, and anti-viral agents. The mushroom itself is nutrition-rich, containing proteins, minerals, vitamins B and D, polysaccharides, and linoleic acids.

Mycelium decompose and consume toxic matter coming from the usual sources: municipal sewage overflow, industrial and agricultural waste, petroleum products—and converts them into harmless by-products and soil-enhancing microbes.

Mushrooms perform a complete, efficient and inexpensive process which includes the following:

1) Mycelium quite literally consume, digest, and decompose toxins and pathogens.
2) Mycelium excrete enzymes and acids, which not only kill harmful bacteria, viruses, and parasites, but also prevents further reproduction of those pathogens.

3) The enzymes also break down chemical bonds at the molecular level, most notably hydrogen-carbon bonds, which are found in petroleum products, pesticides, and toxic chemicals. This chemical breakdown converts these toxic materials into harmless water and carbon dioxide by-products.
4) The mycelium also decompose harmless organic debris such as branches and plant stems. The fungal enzymes enter the plant fibers and break down the plant cells into basic nutrients, which further enrich the soil. This also has an aerating effect on the soil. During the chemical decomposition, micro-cavities, or minute air pockets are created. They hold additional water and act as habitats for beneficial microbial populations. These micro-air and water pockets act to stabilize the soil temperature as well, not only from the additional aeration and moisture, but also from the release of heat, resulting from the natural decomposition of organic matter into carbon dioxide and water. Researchers at Montana State University used mushrooms in a no-till corn field. The mycoflora aggressively decomposed the corn stalk stubble, thus eliminating the need for conventional tilling, while at the same time, increasing the water content and temperature stability of the soil.

Mushrooms are best at breaking down and consuming relatively large molecular toxins. This decomposition process fosters smaller bacterial growth. These relatively smaller, beneficial bacteria are more effective at degrading toxins with smaller molecular weights. This is synergy at the molecular level.

All mushrooms contain mycelium, which degrades organic matter using acids and enzymes. However, each mushroom species has different breakdown characteristics. This said, the most effective use of mushrooms for toxic remediation is to match the right mushroom with the toxin(s) in question. For example: White rot mushrooms se-

Oyster Mushrooms

crete lignin peroxidases, manganese peroxidases, and laccases, which effectively break down hydrogen-carbon bonds found in petrochemicals, as alluded to earlier.

The Washington State Department of Transportation used mushrooms on contaminated soil in a truck maintenance yard. Diesel fuel and oil contaminated 2%, or 20,000 parts per million. They created four piles of contaminated soil, each four feet high, twenty feet long, and eight feet wide. Four cubic yards of pure culture oyster sawdust mushroom spawn was integrated in two piles, while the other two piles were used as controls. After four weeks, the mushrooms matured, produced spores, and started dying. The mature, blooming mushrooms attracted insects, which in turn attracted birds, and a new life cycle began.

An analysis of the mature mushrooms showed no detectable petroleum. That is to say, they decomposed toxic oil and diesel into simple compounds with no toxic residue. The control piles stank of oil while the mushroom piles had no diesel smell whatsoever. The total

White Rot Mushrooms

petroleum contamination in the soil itself was down from 20,000 ppm to 200 ppm in just 8 weeks.

Heavy Metals and Radioactivity

Mushrooms are excellent soil purifiers but they do have their limitations, most notably converting heavy metals and radioactivity into simple, inert compounds. Unfortunately, in these cases the mushrooms perform essentially like large sponges—absorbing heavy metals like PCBs (polychlorinated biphenyls), and radioactivity. Although these are removed from the soil, they are still concentrated in the mushrooms themselves. In these cases the mushrooms most likely would have to be destroyed. Even so, it is far less expensive to remove heavy metals and radioactivity from soil in this manner than the more conventional processes of excavating, shipping, and destroying **all** the soil itself.

Mushrooms as Natural Insecticides

Many mushrooms contain entomopathogenic fungi, which attacks thousands of insect species by boring holes through the insect and spreading the fungi into their organs, ultimately killing the insects. Nature, in its infinite wisdom, blessed many insects with the ability to sniff out and detect mushroom spores, setting off an internal warning to stay away. However, mushroom biologists transformed typical green mold mushrooms into non-sporulating mycelium. This was done by singling out only the mycelium with delayed spore production. They further cultivated those delayed spore mushrooms until they finally got a non-sporulating mycelium. Without spores, the insects cannot detect the danger. In addition, these mycelium also emit insect attractants and feeding stimulants.

A study at Texas A&M University's department of Entomology conducted an experiment exposing termites and fire ants to those non -sporulating mushrooms. The insects were attracted to the mushrooms, ate them, and within two to three weeks died of fungal infection. In addition, the ants brought the mushrooms back to the queen and essentially wiped out the entire colony. These insect-killing entopathogenic fungi can be added to landscapes in the form of wood chips and sawdust in lieu of toxic and expensive insecticides.

The creative land/water manager can use mushrooms by themselves or in conjunction with other modalities, such as constructed marshes with reeds and bulrushes, for a powerful combination of soil/ water clean-up and ecosystem restoration. If the landscape has polluted water, it would be effective to not only plant bulrushes, reeds, water lilies, etc., in the water and along the banks, but also to plant mushrooms along the surrounding land. This will ease the burden on the marsh plants as the rain/stormwater runoff and mud entering the water from the surrounding land will be much cleaner and more conducive to plant and animal life. This further enhances the marsh's ability to purify the water, and will be discussed in more detail throughout the following chapter.

Chapter Five

Water Management

Water purification and storm water solutions

Pervasive depletion and overuse of water supplies, the high capital cost of new large water projects, and worsening ecological damage call for a shift in the way water is valued, used and managed.
– Sandra Postel

Any good management team reduces/eliminates waste, while creating more efficiency. Effective water management is comprehensive, and embraces all or most of the potential cause-effect solutions for a given area. It looks outside property lines or political boundaries and considers water as one large, fluid, interconnected living entity.

The existing paradigm is wasteful, inefficient, and expensive. It degrades water quality and renders areas more susceptible to the deleterious effects of drought and flooding. Despite this, little is being done to change it.

If you need incentives to upgrade your water management policy, there are many from which to choose, including:

1) Increase the value of your property and surrounding areas

2) Reduce water bills and stormwater run-off expense
3) Make your property and surrounding areas more flood and drought resistant
4) Replenish underground aquifers
5) Help purify water systems
6) Create a healthier environment

Like it or not, the weather is becoming more extreme with record heat and cold; heavy rainfall and flooding, followed by extreme drought; an inordinate amount of hurricane force winds, tornadoes, etc. The designs of most buildings and manicured landscapes work **against** existing natural systems. Implementing designs that work **in conjunction with** a given ecosystem are more profitable—on all levels.

Stormwater Runoff

Proficient stormwater management turns problems into an opportunities/benefits. Instead of storm and wastewater runoff dumping directly into our waterways, it could be absorbed, filtered, and fed into already depleted aquifers. This creates more quality drinking water, prevents toxic runoff, and saves taxpayers and municipalities money.

The following case studies will illustrate these benefits on a municipal level, followed by detailed analyses of private residential and small commercial applications. If just a small percentage of residential and commercial property owners incorporated these principles, the need for municipal storm and waste water upgrades previously mentioned most probably would not be necessary. This is solving the problem at the source, rather than treating symptoms. If money talks in this society, why do we continue on this current expensive and destructive path? Regardless of the reasons, political or otherwise, you will now get the tools to help efficiently solve water-related problems.

Stormwater runoff puts an added strain on sewer systems, which are already antiquated and in need of repair. According to a recent study by the American Society of Civil Engineers (ASCE), capital investment needs for the nation's wastewater and stormwater systems are in the hundreds of billions of dollars.

Most municipalities use combined sanitary and stormwater systems. The consensus being it would be less expensive to increase the capacity of one treatment plant rather than to dig up streets and construct different systems for stormwater and sanitary sewers. Combined systems are more prone to overflow during heavy rains: however, stormwater-only systems overflow as well, although to a somewhat lesser extent.

The overflow has nowhere to go except right into the waterways, untreated. Raw sewage ends up in the rivers and beaches, creating health risks and forced closing of those beaches. This also negatively impacts the local fishing industry and other wildlife in the area, not to mention the values of waterfront homes and businesses. Add to this the usual contaminants from the stormwater runoff, including oil, grease and garbage from the roads, pesticides/herbicides and fertilizers from lawns, toxic waste from manufacturing and construction sites, and you have some pretty dirty water. In fact, the EPA identified stormwater as a leading source of pollution in all water types.

Approximately 3 billion gallons of raw sewage flows directly into the Potomac, Rock Creek, and Anacostia Rivers during the many heavy rains throughout the year, according to local water utility D.C. Water. The Tampa Bay Times reported that, according to city officials, some 16.5 million gallons of raw sewage was released into Tampa Bay and Clam Bayou during the heavy August 2015 rains. A month later, the city disclosed that an additional 15 million gallons of partially treated (disinfected, but not filtered) wastewater was released onto the Eckerd College campus, which borders the wastewater treatment plant. Afterward, the city officials were busy passing the buck as to the reasons for the misinformation and lack of communication.

In September, 2016, the heavy rains of tropical storm Hermine created massive stormwater overflows in the same region. This resulted in the dumping of over 170 million gallons of partially treated and raw sewage into Tampa area bays and watersheds. St. Petersburg fisherman, Tyrone Ross said, "You can smell it and see it in the color of the water. It smells like sewage."

City officials inspected over 1,000 homes in the area. They reported nine homes completely destroyed, and 297 with major damage. This was according to Kevin Guthrie, the Pasco County Emergency Services Director.

The Tampa Bay Times reported in November, 2016 that a total of over 200 million gallons of sewage overflowed into Tampa Bay-area waterways, roads, and neighborhoods over the 2-year period from 2015 to 2016. Two months after the 2016 flooding, seabirds were still dying, while researchers have found levels of bacteria 100 to 1,000 times above normal. To make matters worse, two strains of antibiotic-resistant bacteria were singled out by official laboratory tests and researchers at the University of South Florida.

A $45 million short-term fix was proposed by the city of St. Petersburg and a more comprehensive $259 million plan, to be implemented over a 5 year period, was also proposed. These Tampa Bay incidents are microcosm of what is going on nationwide.

The health and economic costs are astronomical. Consider the fishing industry (contaminated fish); medical treatment for chemical and bacteria exposure; waterfront businesses losing customers; loss of tourism; declining property values; contaminated drinking water; clean-up expenses. The list goes on. Figure 6 lists infrastructure improvements needed in 20 states over the next 20 years. It also shows state and federal government funding in an average year. The funding falls far short of what is needed.

The **causes** of the problem are not seriously being addressed, one being overbuilding with unsustainable methods that create massive amounts of stormwater runoff. To follow are practical solutions

State	Drinking Water	Wastewater	Total Funding 2021
Arizona	$15 billion	$1.4 billion	$60.5 million
California	$51 billion	$26.2 billion	$422.8 million
Colorado	$10.2 billion	$4.7 billion	$68.5 million
Connecticut	$4 billion	$4.6 billion	$60.6 million
Florida	$16.5 billion	$18.4 billion	$194.4 million
Georgia	$12.5 billion	$2.7 billion	$80.1 million
Illinois	$21.5 billion	$6.5 billion	$228 million
Indiana	$7.5 billion	$7.2 billion	$110.5 million
Maryland	$9.3 billion	$9.9 billion	$117 million
Michigan	$13 billion	$2.1 billion	$392 million
Minnesota	$7.5 billion	$2.4 billion	$92.3 million
Pennsylvania	$10.2 billion	$8.4 billion	$194.4 million
New Jersey	$8.6 billion	$17.5 billion	$298.9 million
New York	$22.8 billion	$31.4 billion	$444 million
Ohio	$13.4 billion	$17 billion	$236 million
Tennessee	$8.7 billion	$1.7 billion	$84.4 million
Texas	$63 billion	$200 million	$159.7 million
Utah	$4.4 billion	$816 million	$38.5 million
Virginia	$8.1 billion	$6.5 billion	$100.8 million

Figure 6 Drinking water and wastewater infrastructure improvements needed over 20 years and government funding for it. Source: National Utilities Contractors Association

to this problem which **you** can implement on a small or large scale.

The EPA estimates there are some 16,000 wastewater systems in the U.S., 750 of which are combined systems. The overflow of combined systems is estimated at over 850 million gallons per year of untreated water, which spills into rivers, lakes, aquifers, and beaches. Separate wastewater and stormwater systems overflow as well, to the tune of 3-10 million gallons of raw sewage discharge each year.

An EPA study in Santa Monica, CA, concluded that people swimming in front of flowing storm drains are 50% more likely to develop symptoms of illness than people swimming 400 yards from the same drain. These illnesses typically include fever, rashes, earaches, sinus problems, and diarrhea.

The problem only gets worse as more development puts additional strain on antiquated sewers. Where is the debate about this? Where is the outrage? Just how much will people take? Depending on governments to solve water problems is an exercise in futility. The age-old excuse is that it costs too much. But yet it is okay to build a 800 million-dollar sports stadium funded by the local taxpayers, or send hundreds of billions of dollars to other countries.

Sustainable water management is also not being implemented by city and state governments because they say the benefits are not easily quantified and, therefore, projections in overall cost reduction, improved public health, and local economy stimulus are nothing more than educated guesses. That's simply not true.

The cities of Seattle, Washington, and Auburn Hills, Wisconsin, to name a couple, took it upon themselves to implement sustainable water management, study the results, and quantify the financial and environmental benefits.

The 2nd Avenue Street Edge Alternative was put into effect by Seattle Public Utilities to reduce stormwater run-off on a 660 foot residential street block through alternative management techniques. The objective was to reduce as much impervious surface as feasibly possible. Curbs and gutters were taken out and replaced with bioswales, or contoured landscaping with shrubs, trees, and flood tolerant plants. The width of the street was also reduced from 25 feet to 14 feet. The result was an 18% reduction in impervious surface, with a cost of $651,548. When compared to a conventional street/sewer retrofit, it resulted in a 29% cost savings. The largest savings resulted from reduced paving and stormwater infrastructure (sewers and treatment). The environmental results were approximately a 98% reduction in total potential surface water run-off. The site is retaining more than the projected absorption of .75 inches of rain.

Critics may say reducing street width would cause traffic congestion problems. If this did create a problem and redirecting traffic was not an option, there are still other solutions. Pervious pavement, for example, could be used in lieu of conventional asphalt. This would provide drainage results similar to or better than a narrower asphalt street, but keeping the original street width. Yes, this material is more expensive than asphalt, but if you factor in the savings in conventional stormwater infrastructure, it would be a practical, cost-effective solution. Pervious pavement will be discussed more in the Building and Architecture chapter.

The Auburn Hills Subdivision in Southwestern Wisconsin is a development that was initially designed for sustainable water management, as opposed to the Second Ave. Street project, which was retrofitted years after development. This included the use of bio swales and raingardens, as well as higher density cluster homes, which made more land available for drainage purposes. The cost comparisons between this subdivision and conventional building is indicated in Figure 7 on the following page.

One major difference between this subdivision and the previous example was that the lot sizes around each building were much smaller, thereby creating more open, green space. However, what if people do not wish to be squeezed into high density areas and would rather have more land around them? You CAN have it both ways-—good stormwater drainage AND larger lot sizes. This would require

Item	Conventional Development Cost	Auburn Hills LID Cost	Cost Savings	Percent Savings
Site Preparation	$699,250	$533,250	$166,000	24%
Stormwater Management	$664,276	$241,497	$422,779	64%
Site Paving and Sidewalks	$771,859	$584,242	$187,617	24%
Landscaping	$225,000	$240,000	-$15,000	-7%
Total	**$2,360,285**	**$1,598,989**	**$761,396**	

Figure 7 Auburn Hills low Impact development costs compared to conventional stormwater systems

Source: EPA 841-F-07-006

the homeowners to be more proactive with their own property. That is to say, each would use all the means available to capture as close to 100% of their own stormwater runoff as possible. These methods are discussed in detail throughout this book and have minimal to no cost compared to upgraded sewer infrastructure.

Parking Lot Redesigns

The city of Bellingham, Washington, decided to apply sustainable water management to two parking lots in the city—one at City Hall and the other at Bloedel Donovan Park. Rather than build the conventional underground water storage areas, or dry wells, they built rain gardens (see later in this chapter for more detailed rain garden construction methods) to absorb excess runoff.

At the City Hall parking lot, three parking spaces out of 60 were converted into rain gardens. The Bloedel Donovan Park converted a 550-square foot area of the parking lot into a rain garden, which was built near the existing drainage basin. The overflow from this lot would ordinarily run directly into Lake Whatcom, untreated and unfiltered.

The excavation depth was 3-4 feet. There were several 6-inch layers of drainage rocks and gravel, each covered with non-woven geotextile fabric. The top layer of soil was comprised of sand for the drainage capacity and 20-25% organic matter for the absorptive qualities. A variety of native plants with high resistance to both drought and flooding were planted on top. The pollutants from cars, etc., were eaten up by the plants and filtered by the sand and gravel. The city saved approximately 80% on each project while preventing polluted overflow from running into the local waterways. (figure 8)

What was not factored into this analysis was the loss of parking

Project	Conventional Vault Cost	Rain Garden Cost	Cost Savings	% Savings
City Hall	$27,600	$5,600	$22,000	80%
Bloedel Donovan Park	$52,800	$12,800	$40,000	76%

Figure 8 Bellingham Washington parking lot redesigns

spaces, which were redesignated as drainage areas. This requires a cost/benefit analysis—cleaner waterways and lower infrastructure costs vs. extra parking spaces. Once this is determined, the feasibility of the project would become more evident.

The American Society of Civil Engineers considers many "*showcase installations,*" such as the Bellingham Project, to be "*not representative of reasonable designs and costs.*" The ASCE conducted their own comprehensive research, which they felt was a better representation of reasonable designs and costs, and with a more objective point of view. The Turkey Creek Basin in the Missouri River Northeast Industrial district of Kansas City was the object of the study.

The objective was to quantify the cost/savings/benefits of combining "green" infrastructure with traditional sewer systems. by determining optimal combinations of rain gardens of varying sizes combined with the appropriate size and length sewer lines for maximum cost reduction, and the most effective stormwater runoff/pollution control. That is to say, reduce or eliminate stormwater overflow at a lower cost and with less pollution entering the waterways. Several scenarios itemizing all costs and stormwater capture volume are presented and compared:

1. Conventional sewer lines only - Alternative 1
2. Conventional sewer lines with smaller pipe diameter and length combined with raingardens of varying sizes to ab sorb the excess stormwater - Alternative 2
3. Raingarden number and size option 1 - large raingardens
4. Raingarden number and size option 2 - more, but smaller raingardens

A cost breakdown was used to demonstrate the effectiveness of rain gardens in lieu of conventional sewer lines as an efficient, non-polluting stormwater-management method. Some figures in the charts may not appear to be exact due to rounding up large numbers in initial cost calculations.

The subject covers a 5,554-acre area in the Turkey Creek Basin. The largest zoned use is single family medium density, which was 806 acres. The next largest use was parks and open space, approximately 748 acres.

Figure 9 (Alternative 1, next page) itemizes conventional-size sewer line costs, designed for a yearly stormwater overflow volume of 480 million gallons. Additional costs to the actual sewer lines is outfall, which includes double box sewers, earthwork, odor control, and water level monitoring. The total cost for outfall is $5,000,000, which is the same for all alternatives. Site adjustment for traffic routing was calculated at .5% of base construction costs.

Conventional Sewer Stormwater Costs
Alternative 1

Tunnel Diameter (ft.)	Length (ft.)	Volume (cubic ft.)	Volume (1,000 gal.)	Total Cost ($ millions)
26	13,400	7,114,445	53,220	101
20	7,880	2,475,573	18,519	38
15	9,440	1,668,184	12,479	32
12	21,410	2,421,412	18,113	59
Total	**52,130**		**102,330**	**230**

Number of shafts	16
Number of uses	3
Subtotal cost	230
Outfall and site adjustment for outfall	5
Base construction costs (BCC)	236
Site adjustment for traffic routing	1
Total construction costs (TCC)	237
Land (5% of BCC)	1
Engineering, administration, inspection	59
Total capital costs	372
Present value—operations, maintenance	13
Present value other costs	110
Total Present Value Cost	**385**

Figure 9 Conventional stormwater sewer costs in the Turkey Creek Basin, Kansas City , Missouri

Base Cost Smaller Tunnel Sizes
Alternative 2

Tunnel Diameter (ft.)	Length (ft.)	Volume (cubic ft.)	Volume (1,000 gal.)	Total cost ($millions)
20	12,000	4,156,324	31,090	63
20	5,000	1,570,795	11,750	24
15	6,000	1,060,287	7,931	20
12	15,000	1,696,459	12,690	41
Total	**38,000**		**63,461**	**149**

Number of shafts	16
Number of uses	3
Subtotal cost	149
Outfall and site adjustment for outfall	5
Base construction costs	54
Site adjustment (traffic routing)	1
Total construction costs (TCC)	155
Land (.5% of BCC)	1
Engineering, administration, inspection	39
Project contingency	49
Total capital costs	244
PV operations and maintenance	9
Total Present Value Cost	**253**

Figure 10 Using smaller tunnel sizes in conjunction with raingardens to make up the difference in stormwater capacity

Rain Garden Option 1 – Larger Raingardens

	# raingardens	Cost ($ millions)	Volume (thousand gal.)
Water capture alternative 1			102,330
Water capture alternative 2			63,464
Difference			38,867
Volume retention/raingarden			**1.60**
Raingardens needed to absorb difference	24,506		
Present value (PV) cost per raingarden		.0045	
PV cost per 1000 gallons captured		.0028	
Total PV cost of larger raingardens		**110**	
Total PV cost for alternative 1		385	
Total PV cost for alternative 2		363	
Difference in PV cost between alternatives 1 and 2		22	

Figure 11 Costs of larger but fewer raingardens

Outfall combined with actual tunnel costs equals base construction costs. Adding site adjustment to the base construction costs gives the total construction costs. Other costs, including land, engineering, project contingencies, and salvage value, are also itemized in figures 9 and 10 (alternatives 1 and 2) at the bottom. Raingarden options 1 and 2 are shown in figures 11 and 12 respectively.

As tunnel diameters increase, the cost per 1,000 gallons of water decreases. These economies of scale were factored in to the conven-

Rain Garden Option 2 – More, Smaller Raingardens

	# raingardens	Cost ($ millions)	Volume (thousand gal.)
Water capture alternative 1			102,330
Water capture alternative 2			63,464
Difference			38,867
Volume retention/raingarden			**.75**
Raingardens needed to absorb difference	51,822		
Present value (PV) cost per raingarden		.0019	
PV cost per 1000 gallons captured		.0025	
Total PV cost-smaller raingardens		**97**	
Total PV cost for alternative 1		385	
Total PV cost for alternative 2		350	
Difference in PV cost between alternative s 1 and 2		35	

Figure 12 Costs of more, smaller raingardens

tional sewer costs. The additional excavation costs associated with the larger diameter pipes were minimal.

The total present value costs for alternative 1 (conventional tunnel sizes) was $385 million. Figure 10 (alternative 2) shows the lower costs associated with smaller conventional sewer lines. The total cost of these tunnels alone was $253 million. Rain gardens were constructed in addition to the smaller sewer tunnels to compensate for the reduced capacity and resulting overflow. These rain garden costs the reduced capacity and resulting overflow. These rain garden costs will be added to the smaller tunnel costs later on. The figures were derived from the Overflow Control Program Basis of Cost Manual of Kansas City, MO, WSD.

There are two rain garden options to be used in conjunction with smaller tunnel sizes. Option 1 in figure 11 shows the costs and absorptive efficacy of larger raingardens. A total of 24,506 raingardens with a total cost on $110 million were needed to absorb the difference in additional wastewater created from using smaller pipes. This method had a present value cost saving of $22,000,000 compared to using conventional sewer lines only. (alternative 1)). The discount rate of 5% was used to determine present value costs. The assumed lifespan was 50 years.

Option 2 in figure 12 used more raingardens (51,822) but of smaller sizes than those in option 1. The net stormwater capture was the same, as both absorbed equal amounts of water (38,867,000 gallons).

The larger rain gardens in option 1 were 12' wide by 20' long by 3' deep, each having the capacity to absorb 1,585 gallons of runoff. The smaller raingardens in option 2 were 5' wide by 20' long and 1' deep. The volume retention capacity per raingarden of this size was 750 gallons. The cost to build a greater number of smaller rain gardens was $97 million (figure 12) compared to the $110 million cost to build larger but fewer rain gardens (figure 11). Again, each method captured the same amount of stormwater.

The Bottom Line

This and other studies clearly demonstrate the viability of constructing raingardens as a partial replacement of traditional stormwater sewer lines. The most cost-effective method was to use a greater number of smaller-size raingardens (compared to fewer but larger raingardens) in lieu of additional stormwater tunnels. This saved $22,000,000 compared to conventional stormwater tunnels only. The net effects would be greatly reduced or completely eliminated sewage overflows, cleaner waterways, underground aquifer replenishing, and major cost reduction.

It is obvious that large, centralized systems are often times inefficient and expensive. Higher transport costs reduce profitability. Whether it's food, stormwater, wastewater, electricity, or drinking water, carrying anything over long distances typically negates the economies of scale associated with large centralized systems such as mega-farms, power plants, storm/waste water transport networks, and the like.

This could all change, but the United States, and the rest of the world seems to be heading in the opposite direction, towards more centralization, and therefore more control over the people. Decentralization on the other hand creates more self-reliance and independence.

The solutions, therefore, lie more and more with individuals and how they understand and interact with their immediate environment. Few or none of these water overflow problems would exist if property owners and managers—from single family to large commercial facilities—would practice more comprehensive and synergistic land/water management as outlined in this book. The cost is significantly less and with greater far benefit than most conventional methods.

Stormwater Costs

Stormwater drainage can be a costly expense for most commercial properties and, to a somewhat lesser extent, residential properties. Water drainage in residential areas is more of a flooding issue than direct sewer expense.

Stormwater fees are based on the square feet of impervious surface on the property. Depending upon the municipality, there is a specific rate charged per square foot per month, which is based on ERU's, or Equivalent Residential Units. Each ERU is equal to one thousand square feet (1,000 sq. ft.) of impervious surface.

In the District of Columbia, for example, each ERU is charged \$2.67 per month. If a residential property there has 2,700 square feet of roof surface and another 1,900 square feet of sidewalk, driveway, and patio, the combined impervious surface equals 4,600 square feet. The unit rate would be 3.8, as the square footage of impervious surface is between 3,100 and 7.000 square feet. See figure 13. The stormwater fee would be \$10.15 per month (3.8 X \$2.67).

For all other properties, such as businesses and large multi-family properties, the stormwater fee will be charged \$2.67 per month for each 1,000 square feet of impervious area on their lot, reduced to the nearest 100 square feet. For example, the monthly stormwater fee for a commercial property with 26,500 square feet of impervious area would be calculated as follows: 26,500 square feet / 1,000 square feet = 26.5 X \$2.67 = \$70.76 per month.

Most municipalities have discount programs to cut these expenses by half or more if you demonstrate sustainable designs that reduce/eliminate water runoff. These individual savings certainly add up, but these designs also lessen the need for long term infrastructure improvements due to the massive reduction in stormwater volume. That is to say, less of your tax dollars being spent on unnecessary sewer enlargement projects. The benefits are even more significant if you take into account the long-term effects of aquifer replenishing and pollution reduction.

Other property owners/managers, builders and city planners, etc. should take notice, if for no other reason than to help their bottom lines. Now you helped create a shift from centralized, expensive and inefficient systems to a more integrated, synergistic approach. All this translates into higher appraised values, increased marketability, better lease opportunities, and healthier environments.

Typically, there is little or no planning on the developers' part to deal effectively with stormwater runoff. In the southeastern United

Figure 13 District of Columbia Stormwater Unit Rates

Square Feet	**Unit Rate**
100—600	.6
700—2,000	1
2,100—3000	2.4
3,100—7,000	3.8
7,100—11,000	8.6
11,000 and above	13.5

States for example, new developments usually construct "retention ponds," which are nothing more than large, bare holes in the ground placed in the middle of a subdivision. These otherwise dry, parched mud holes are full during the rainy season, and often overflow given the lack of vegetation and organic matter in the soil. This also creates the perfect breeding ground for mosquitoes. Even here a little creative management could go a long way. These could be turned into balanced, regenerating, self-purifying ponds with the introduction of certain aquatic and shoreline plants. (See the Lakes chapter for more on the role of aquatic plants in transforming polluted lakes into clear, balanced ecosystems.)

Anyone who is serious about solving water problems (too much/too little/too dirty) should not only look at potential solutions in their immediate area, but also consider how land is being developed on a larger scale (subdivisions, shopping centers, industrial sites…) and lobby on behalf of the ecosystems that are being systematically destroyed, at everyone's expense. (See the Legal Rights of Ecosystems chapter on how laws are being enforced around the country, and world, to give those systems legal standing.)

Rain Gardens – Solving Your Own Water Problems

Rain gardens are an efficient, aesthetic, and balanced approach to mitigating floods/drought and would virtually eliminate the need for retention ponds or expanded sewer systems. They are natural drainage/irrigation systems that absorb flood waters while retaining water during sustained drought. They also filter out contaminates and toxins from the water runoff that would otherwise make their way into the rivers, lakes, streams, and oceans. Fertilizers, lead, pesticides, and oil are absorbed and purified to a large degree by the microorganisms and deep rooted plants of rain gardens.

The cheapest place to hold water is in the soil. Rich soil containing over 2% organic matter can reduce irrigation by 75% compared to soil with less than 1% organic matter. Put another way, for every 1% of organic matter content, the soil can hold approximately16,000 gallons of additional water per acre of soil down to one foot deep. Increasing the organic matter content from 1 to 2 % essentially doubles the amount of water retaining capabilities.

The increased absorptive qualities significantly reduce runoff, soil erosion, and flooding. Most developments today have little organic matter in the soil, as builders typically clear-cut and bulldoze entire tracts of land, leaving behind a barren landscape devoid of trees, humus and quality topsoil. The resulting flooding problems shouldn't be surprising. You can be more proactive and take matters into your own hands by implementing these inexpensive, yet efficient systems into your own property.

One of the first steps is to analyze the soil, and its ability to absorb water. Steps should be taken to increase the organic content of the soil, as absorptive qualities are directly related to soil composition and plant types. Rain gardens, like any effective management technique, turn problems (flood/drought) into solutions (water retention, overflow prevention, and water storage for later use in drought conditions).

The benefits are many, and the cost is minimal. I have seen

countless properties where the land slopes down towards the building. Sudden downpours invariably create some degree of flooding, either entering the building or in the form of standing water around the foundation, which could/will lead to cracks and seepage. Either way, it is not good. Many resort to putting in an actual sewer, which connects to the main line at the street. This is a major expense, which requires digging up the back and side yards to lay the piping. A properly designed rain garden (in some severe cases, more than one may be needed to control any overflow) could essentially do the same job for pennies on the dollar. The other benefits would be more irrigation for the surrounding landscape, increased value/ marketability, and an aesthetic improvement over a sewer in your back yard.

Again, this is about self-reliance, working creatively with the land rather than against it. Anyone who studies the martial arts will tell you that the key to defeating your opponent is to go with his/her strengths and use them to your advantage, redirecting rather than resisting them outright. In the case of water, we are redirecting the flow to the rain garden where it dissipates, purifies and re-circulates.

Building Your Own Natural Sewer, Irrigation, and Water Purification System

The first step is to sketch the property. This includes building locations, topography, vegetation, sloping or low-lying areas, and the natural path of water flow during heavy rains, including standing water. Raingardens should be built on or around the lower lying areas where stormwater tends to collect.

The next step is to decide how much water runoff you want to contain. This runoff comes primarily from impervious surfaces like the rooftops, sidewalks, driveways, parking lots, etc. You will need to decide what percentage of this runoff you want to contain. In order to capture all the runoff from the roof, driveway, etc., the formula would be total impervious surface square footage (roof, etc.) divided by 20 for a 6" deep garden to capture 1" of rain. For example, if the building is 2,000 square feet and you just wanted to capture the runoff from the back half of the roof, the formula would be 1000 divided by 20 equals 50. That is to say you would need a 50-square foot garden that is 6" deep to capture all the water from the back side of the roof during a rainstorm producing 1" of water. A 6" rain garden in this example is actually 12" below grade. The actual fill is 6" deep while the ponding area above it is another 6". The ponding area is the depth from the surrounding land to the top of the raingarden fill.

Since you already determined the best location for the rain garden, now you can try to divert as much water to that location as necessary. PVC pipes can be connected to your downspouts to transport water away from the building and toward the rain garden. If the ground is level, a slight slope can be dug so gravity pulls the water away. The last section of piping nearest to the raingarden could be perforated to provide a more even flow..

Look at the sketch of the landscape to ascertain the best location. If water is settling at a certain area far enough from the house, you would probably want to build one there. If the water is standing too close to the building, it should be diverted away and to a lower area. This can be done by building shallow swales, which may or may not follow the contour of the land. The width and depth depends entirely on the amount of water to be diverted and/or absorbed. Some are as small a just a few inches deep with the width being about 2-3 times that of the depth. They should be level so the water flows evenly.

Now you can start digging the rain garden so that the final filled-in area is 6 inches below grade, another 6 inches deep with pervious fill, and 50 square feet in total area. Create a contour line around the perimeter. The back side should normally be higher and built up with any excess dirt. Planting shrubs and placing rocks along this back wall reinforces it and prevents overflow. Sometimes more than one garden is required to catch any overflow. If this happens, follow the overflow pattern and build another, or make the existing garden deeper or wider.

Water may tend to puddle more in some areas than others due to different soil types, in which case you may have to excavate additional dirt and replace it with more porous compost, sand, hummus, etc. Or, you could move the garden to a nearby area with better-suited soil. Berms can be constructed to redirect water to the new garden.

We installed two raingardens on a property in North Georgia, where the soil consists mainly of clay. We constructed a typical garden with a 6-inch ponding area. (This is the depth measured from the top of the surrounding berm to the top of the recessed raingarden soil.) We dug another 6 inches down, filled it with porous raingarden soil, and planted the appropriate vegetation. After several rainstorms, it became apparent that the clay underneath the garden was too impervious—resulting in frequent overflow. The only solution was to excavate more clay from the bottom, making the total depth 24 inches. This solved the problem.

It is always best to analyze your soil to determine the required depth. The depths typically range from 25 inches for impervious, clay -type under soil, to 6 inches for relatively coarse, pervious undersoil.

The key is to create an area that is highly absorptive. The raingarden fill should be a combination of coarse and fine-textured dirt, with the coarser material placed on the surface layers to maximize absorption, especially during flash flooding situations. Please note that top soil does not work well. It is too fine and does not absorb well. It is best to use a lot of organic matter such as compost, possibly mixed with some coarse sand. Then mix this all together with some of the soil that was just dug out. It is also a good idea to use pebbles or small stones at the entrance of the garden to slow down water flow and thus prevent any unnecessary erosion.

Raingarden Plants

Common Name	Scientific Name	Moisture	Sun
Black Eyed Susan	Rudbekia herta	dry-moist	full-part
Goldenrod	Solidago patula	moist-wet	full-part
Arrowood	Viburnum dentatum	dry-wet	full sun/shade
Rushes	Juncus effusus	moist-wet	full-part
Indigo	Baptisia australis	dry-wet	full
Copper Irises	Iris fulva	moist-wet	full
Redtwig Dogwood	Cornus sericea	dry-moist	full-part
Sweetbay Magnolia	Magnolia virginiana	moist	full-part
Swamp Milkweed	Asciep incarnata	moist-wet	full-sun/shade
Turtlehead	Chelone giabra	moist-wet	full-part
Inkberry	Ilex gladbra	moist-wet	full-part
Bald Cypress	Taxodium distichum	Dry-wet	full

Figure 14 Raingarden plants with moisture and sun requirements

What to Plant

The plants you use will depend upon your local climate and the conditions within the rain garden itself. Some areas may have more sun or shade and the soil moisture may vary as well.

The ideal plants have deep roots, preferably with a balanced blend of deciduous, perennials, and evergreens. Depending on where the garden is, you will want to get plants that thrive in any of six interrelated conditions: full sun, part sun, shade, dry, moist (most of the time), and wet (up to several inches of standing water for prolonged periods). Figure 14 shows a partial list of rain garden plants suited for various types of sun exposures and water requirements in the Midwestern and Southern United States.

The rain gardens not only contain/absorb floodwaters, they can also act as irrigation systems. You may have an area of grass or plants near the rain garden that gets full sun all day and requires regular watering. Just by being in close proximity to the rain garden, this area would require much less, or no additional watering. Besides the obvious and immediate benefits, one should take comfort in the fact that all this water that is collected and absorbed is naturally filtered and purified, while replenishing the under ground aquifers. Fossil aquifers, upon which many towns and cities depend for their water supplies, are non-replenishing, except for whatever surface absorption takes place.

In addition, the polycultural plants typically found in rain gardens create small ecosystems which contribute to the health and stability of the area. This diversification attracts predator insect species, such as ladybugs, which eat aphids and control the pest insect population. The taller plants create shade for the smaller, more sun-sensitive plants and add to the biodiversity of the area.

Needless to say, there are water crises around the world today, including the sinkhole problems alluded to earlier. Efficient, effective non-intrusive and inexpensive water management can go a long way in solving many water problems.

If money dictates policy in this world, why aren't significant steps being taken to protect the aquifers and solve water problems at the source? One would think reducing infrastructure and flood/pollution remediation expenses for municipalities would be a catalyst for implementing new city or state water and building codes that reinforce rather than deplete aquifers. But that is not the case in places across the country where building is booming under outdated standards.

One has to wonder how the "landscape" would change if just 25% of the buildings had raingardens that captured 80 to 100% of the property's stormwater. How many billions of gallons of water would enter the aquifer system rather than overloading the sewer system

Figure 14A Small North Georgia raingarden

and dumping polluted water into the bays and rivers? That would at once help solve sinkhole, water shortage, and stormwater overflow problems.

It usually takes events of catastrophic proportions to change anything, such as is the case in California. Here, there were mandatory reductions in water use, up to 25% in some areas, and complete water shutoff in others, including prestigious subdivisions. The depletion of the California aquifer has gotten so bad that the ground is literally sinking as a result of the lowered underground water table.

According to the Center of Investigative Reporting, some places are sinking more than one foot per year. Joseph Poland of the U.S. Geological Survey documented that between 1955 and 1977 parts of the San Joaquin Valley sunk by more than 30 feet. Farmers started pumping underground water for agriculture on the 1920s, and sure enough, by the 1930s scientists first noticed the land was sinking.

According to a NASA report released in August, 2015, parts of the San Juaquin Valley are now sinking at the fastest rate ever recorded. In order to survive the recent California drought, many farmers drilled new, deeper wells to irrigate their fields. In 2014, part of the southern San Juaquin Valley near the city of Corcoran sunk by more than 13 inches in just an 8-month period. That same area sunk three feet between 2006 and 2010.

Kansas Aquifers Drop Over 100 Feet

There is a looming threat to food production in the U.S. central plains as the underground water supply for irrigation farming is running out. The primary water source for central plains farming is the High Plains-Ogallala Aquifer, where water levels have been precipitously dropping since the advent of deep well irrigation in the post world War II era. Approximately 90% of the water withdrawn from this aquifer is for irrigation farming.

Water level tracking began in 1958, and by 1976 the Kansas Geological survey reported the water table dropped by 134 feet in the Little Rock area of Kansas. The mean decline across 12 counties in Southwest Kansas was 103 feet.

Water pumping is a means of survival for farmers. They have no choice if they want to continue farming. The general business community consensus is that aquifer decline is necessary for economic growth and that sustainable levels of groundwater use would mean no economic growth. This is better known as a situation of "controlled decline." That is to say, mortgage the future and continue with business as usual. The debate about water scarcity has been ongoing for decades. Kansas Governor Sam Brownback said in 2012, "A regret I have is that more has not been done to preserve the Ogallala Aquifer.... We have no future without water."

An Oxford University Press paper entitled, *Race to the Bottom (of the Well): Groundwater in an Agricultural Production Treadmill* states:

> Groundwater depletion in this region persists in the presence of long-term technological modernization. One would be hard-pressed to find another agricultural region where modernization is broader or deeper. Agriculture in this region is at the vanguard in adoption rates of the most advanced, efficient production technologies

This statement reflects the general consensus in the region, that "The only way out of the ecological crisis is by going further into the process of modernization." That premise is embraced even though it clearly does not work well enough.

Why modernization technology does not solve the water depletion problems can in part be traced back to the economic business model. Farmers are always looking to produce more yield per acre while keeping costs at a minimum. Capital intensive technologies such as center pivot pumps produce more efficient irrigation systems and thereby lower costs. However, in order to cover the capital expenditure, production must be expanded, thereby increasing water pumping from the aquifer. The banks are happy to accommodate as they issue more loans to service which the farmers pay back from their higher production revenues.

The farm insurance industry and government subsidies programs provide further inducement for expanded production, such as irrigated crops (using groundwater) being categorized as less risky and with lower premiums than others. This is added incentive for more irrigated crop production. Sometimes farmers make more money from failed crops, as insurance companies pay farmers for their typical yield under good conditions even though the current crop may have failed.

The following sentence from *Race to the Bottom, Groundwater in the Agricultural Production Treadmill* pretty much sums it up. "Subsidies, in this sense, distort the information the farmers receive from the ecosystem while promoting capital intensive expansion in production, putting further spin on the treadmill." Government farm subsidies in Kansas alone between 1995 and 2020 totaled $24.6 billion.

The question remains, why aren't more **non-capital intensive** methods being used which **recharge** aquifers rather than **deplete** them? This High Plains-Ogallala aquifer lies beneath much of the Midwestern United States, which includes a lot of developed (residential, commercial, industrial) land. Where is the discussion about sustainable building and development methods that reduce flooding while recharging aquifers? That would go a long way in raising aquifer levels and providing farmers with more irrigation water. But no, the mantra is always that technology will save the day. Why? Most probably because a few people/corporations stand to profit financially,

Today, the Southwest Kansas Groundwater Management District (GMD) is the regional water authority for those 12 counties covering approximately 8,342 square miles in Southwestern Kansas. Their primary function is to monitor aquifer levels and preside over the allocation of water for irrigation farming. It is in my opinion that if the agencies such as building, construction permitting, code enforcement, water management. etc. worked in concert across county and state lines rather than as separate entities, the common goal of water abundance could be achieved. For example, if the Kansas Groundwater Management District had a say in new development protocols, each new building development would have to absorb a much higher percentage of its own stormwater runoff, which by default, would raise aquifer levels. This is not to mention the other benefits of flood reduction, and lower stormwater infrastructure expenditure for things like excavation, underground piping, land purchase, sewer maintenance, etc.

Florida-Georgia Water Wars

For the better part of the last 3 decades the state of Florida has argued before the courts that Georgia was siphoning off too much water from their main water supply—the Chattahoochee River and Lake Altoona. The Chattahoochee river turns into the Apalachicola River and flows directly into Apalachicola Bay in the Florida panhandle. They claimed salt water was encroaching upon and killing the estuary ecosystems due to diminished fresh water flow from the north. This in turn hurt their fishing industry, most notably the oyster beds. Shannon Hartsfield, president of the local seafood workers' association said the region went from more than 300 working oyster boats when he was a kid to about a dozen today. "This used to be a breeding ground, you know, for shrimp and fish and crabs," he says. "It's all changed up drastically." Many other fishing-related businesses have since gone out of business due to this shortage of fresh water flow.

The state of Florida sued Georgia for using up too much water from these sources due to their uncontrolled and unsustainable development, especially, but not limited to, the ever growing Cobb county and Cartersville areas. This case obviously had merit and legal standing as it eventually worked its way up to the Supreme Court. In August of 2021, the Supreme Court justices unanimously ruled in favor of Georgia, saying that Florida did not show adequate proof of damage, and that the benefits of apportioning water flow would substantially outweigh the harm that may result.

To their credit, the state of Georgia implemented some water saving measures, especially with regard to farming practices. This included the implementation of more efficient irrigation methods and placing a moratorium on drilling new wells. Absent from the debate, however, was any serious discussion about implementing new building development protocols, as the sprawling suburbs of the Atlanta metro area are rapidly expanding in all directions. Like General Sherman's relentless march from Atlanta to the sea, natural regenerating water retention and purification ecosystems are being indiscriminately paved over leaving flood/drought prone areas in its wake.

There are solutions, such as those outlined in this chapter. However, they do not require massive government contracts, corporate subsidies, tax increases or high tech patents since they are relatively inexpensive and low tech. As such, they do not get the headlines in the so-called news media. Looking at these water issues from an objective, strategic point of view, wouldn't it make the most sense to solve two problems (flood and drought) at the same time with minimal expense rather than investing billions in a project that alleviates symptoms rather than addressing the real source of the problem?

The world's water supplies are turning into privatized commodities and sold for profit by global corporations. More control over life-giving natural resources means less freedom for everyone else. Political leaders should be discussing real solutions to create water abundance and all the benefits afforded to all. Given the nature of politics in the world, this probably will not happen. So, it is up to you, the individual property owner/manager/land steward, to start in your own backyard. Once enough people notice the real, tangible benefits a groundswell of change may (will) take effect.

Freshwater Marshes and Wetlands for Water Purification and Aquifer Replenishing

Marshes, or wetlands, are nature's answer to today's global water dilemma, be it too much in the form of flooding, not enough as in severe drought, or highly contaminated and toxic. The complex systems that make up these wetlands are invaluable for stormwater drainage, water purification, highly absorptive organic soil formation, and aquifer recharging.

Given these solutions to water-related problems marshes provide, it would make sense to utilize them more effectively. This would include restricting the arbitrary filling in and paving over natural wetland areas in new development projects. as the benefits they provide far outweigh the monetary profits gained by construction companies profiting from buying inexpensive land due to the high water table and soft terrain. Also, property owners/managers of existing buildings should be incentivized to absorb as close to 100% of their stormwater runoff as possible. This can be done by constructing marshes on their own property. More on how to construct a marsh on

Figure 15 Bulrush marsh

a large or small scale is detailed later in this chapter.

Smaller residential backyard marshes/wetlands are also effective in areas that are wet or even below water most of the year. They can turn a water problem into a creative solution—transforming a mosquito-breeding flood-prone area into a balanced, water-purifying ecosystem that absorbs water through periods of heavy rain and retains moisture during drought. The aesthetic benefits also turn an eyesore into a lush, maintenance-free, self-regulating water system.

In commercial application, the marsh can also double as a recreational/retreat area for employees or used for outdoor corporate events. It could act as a buffer from other buildings or roads, and as such, will add considerable value to the property.

Marshes as Water Purifiers

Water pollution is encroaching upon the world's water supplies like a malignant cancer. The quick fix of choice appears to be dumping more chemicals, such as chlorine, ammonia, and the like into the affected areas. This has its place, but not in lieu of other cleaner, inexpensive, and effective water-purifying systems that produce no harmful side effects.

Dr. Kaethe Seidel, head of the former Limnology Group of the Max Planck Institute realized the benefits of marsh plants some sixty years ago. Her advocacy for the use of bulrushes and other aquatic plants in water purification earned her the nickname Bulrush Kate (Die Binzen Kaethe).

Dr. Seidel was a pioneer in wastewater and water purification, not with high technology, but with the controlled use of aquatic plants and natural systems. In 1953, the general consensus was that plants could not thrive in polluted waters, much less eliminate toxins. She experimented with constructed wetlands to treat wastewater—industrial, agricultural, municipal sludge, landfills, etc. The plants she used effectively removed heavy metals, cleaned oil spills, and killed bacteria and viruses while also balancing the pH. In some cases the water was turned into pure drinking water. Experiments conducted at the Gelsenkirchen Hygiene Institute in Urach, Germany concluded that rushes significantly reduce or completely eliminate E. coli, coliform bacteria, and salmonella.

There are numerous examples of constructed wetlands worldwide that are used to treat wastewater—with good results. It is interesting to note that their use is not more widespread, as these are cost -effective, efficient, non-invasive systems that solve water problems.

Dr. Seidel was somewhat shunned by high-tech engineers who would rather be recognized for their own scientific innovations than give all the credit to a bulrush or reed. According to her:

> Men always reach for technology, for development. They insist it will bring us into higher levels of progress. They haven't the patience to work with slow-growing plants, nor do they understand natural cycles as women do. They see my work as farming, not engineering, so they go away and return to their machinery.

One of the best water purifiers is the bulrush (Schoenoplectus lacustris). They enrich the soil with humus and beneficial bacteria. They also create antibiotics which kill molds, fungi, bacteria, and viruses.

The common reed (Phragmites communis Trin) dries and breaks down sludge into basic minerals. Other plants found to be effective water purifiers are water hyacinths, sunflowers, cattails, water mint (Mentha aquat) water plaintain (Allisma plan) soft rush (Juncus eff) and yellow flag (Iris pseudo).

One study by R. Kickuth of the Gottenheim Institute for Soil Science documented the removal of hydrocarbons such as phenol and its derivatives from wastewater. In the three-year experiment, phenol was added to well water on a regular basis at concentrations of 100mg/liter. Rushes were found to have removed 100% of the phenol when the water was tested each season. One by-product of the phenol removal was the formation of beneficial hummus, which enhanced the soil biomass. Other toxic phenol derivatives were added to the water, which included p-cresol, xylol, hydroquinone, resorcinol, pyrocatechol, and Pyrolgallol, B. They were added in quantities far exceeding lethal doses for fish. These toxic compounds were completely removed by the rushes.

The EPA report Aquaculture Systems for Wastewater Treatment documented the use of water hyacinths and their water purifying characteristics: "Wetland systems can achieve high removal efficiencies of BOD (biological oxygen demand), SS (suspended solids), trace organics, heavy metals, and nitrogen. Their potential may exceed that achieved with mechanical treatment systems."

An Indian study at the Institute of Rock Mechanics and the Vellore Institute of Technology found similar water purifying effects of water hyacinths. The removal efficiencies of BOD and COD (chemical oxygen demand) were 99% and 80% respectively. When demand for oxygen is reduced, oxygen levels naturally rise. The importance of oxygen in this process cannot be overstated, which will become more evident later. They also observed an 87% efficiency in the reduction of ammonia, and an 84% nitrogen removal efficiency in just 8 weeks. The increase in dissolved oxygen in the water from photosynthetic activity created favorable conditions for the bacterial breakdown of other contaminants. The study further revealed high reduction rates for heavy metals including cadmium, mercury, and arsenic, and the absorption of organic substances such as phenol, formaldehyde, and acetic acid.

A study at the University of California, Davis proved the cost-effectiveness of aquatic plant-based (water hyacinths) wastewater treatment compared to conventional treatment. The conclusions were a capital cost savings of 42%, and 47% in energy savings.

The Santee River, California water reclamation facility experimented with the use of bulrushes, reeds, and cattails in the purification of wastewater. They constructed four separate beds, one each with bulrushes, cattails, and reeds, with the fourth bed remaining unvegetated. Figure 16 shows the wastewater contaminants entering the beds, and their removal by each of the three plant types and the non-vegetated control bed.

Two major pollutants in our water today are nitrogen and phos-

Figure 16 Santee River Mean Effluent Levels Before Treatment (all values in milligrams per liter—mg/L)

Total Nitrogen (TN)	27.8
Total Inorganic Nitrogen ((TIN)	25
Ammonia (N)	24.7
Biologic Oxygen Demand (BOD)	118.3
Total Suspended Solids (SS)	57.3

Ammonia accounted for just under 90% of the total Nitrogen flowing into the beds, and was reduced as follows:

Bed Type	**Bulrushes**	**Reeds**	**Cattails**	**Unvegetated**
Ammonia Removal	94%	78%	28%	11%

phorus. The levels are artificially elevated through agricultural, wastewater, and stormwater runoff containing animal excretion/decomposition, detergents, fertilizers, pesticides, oil, etc. The process of decomposition and other chemical reactions triggered by these substances uses up a lot of oxygen. Water with decreased oxygen levels cannot properly sustain life, and this throws the whole biological system out of whack, including the health of plants, fish, mammals, and many types of small organisms, most of which are important to the balance, health, and purification of water bodies.

There is a dead zone in the Gulf of Mexico, which is approximately 6.500 square miles, beginning at the mouth of the Mississippi River. All the runoff from farms, wastewater, etc., ends up there, depleting oxygen levels. Referring to the Gulf of Mexico, The National Oceanic and Atmospheric Administration says, "Dead zones, also called hypoxia areas, are caused by nutrient runoff from agricultural and other human activities in the watershed and are highly affected by river discharge and nitrogen loads."

How Wetland Plants Purify Water

Nitrogen and phosphorus are the major contaminants in our water supplies, as mentioned before. An overview of wetland plants' roles in the nitrogen removal process is explained below.

Nitrogen has several forms—ammonia, nitrate, and nitrite. Wetland plants effectively remove ammonia (the primary component of nitrogen) through several processes:

1) **Nitrification** – This is a two-step process by which nitrogen compounds, primarily ammonia (NH_3), are converted to nitrite (NO_2) by ammonia-oxidizing bacteria. The nitrite is then converted to nitrate (NO_3) by heterotrophic bacteria (bacteria using carbon as an energy source). The nitrification process requires oxygen, with the levels of dissolved oxygen in the water being proportional to nitrification efficiency. The plants help this process by releasing oxygen into the surrounding water via photosynthesis, and into the sediment through the root structure. These increased oxygen levels help stimulate nitrifying bacteria and ammonia oxidation.

2) **Denitrification** reduces nitrate to nitrous oxide gasses (subsequently released into the atmosphere) through anaerobic (without oxygen) bacterial activity. These bacteria use nitrates instead of oxygen for their respiration.

Rushes and other wetland plants also enrich the soil with humus. This helps populate the soil with beneficial bacteria and microbes, which remove soluble organic compounds by decomposing them both aerobically and anaerobically. That is to say, with or without oxygen. While both surface and bottom areas are oxygenated through photosynthesis, surface waters are even more aerobic due to the additional oxygen intake from air being diffused into the water. These two different zones perform separate functions in removing contamination.

Oxygen plays an important role in most all wetland water purifying processes as it supports beneficial bacteria and microbes, which breakdown and oxidize harmful compounds. A study by the Office of

Water Programs at California State University, Sacramento stated "the primary limiting agent for nitrification in wetlands is dissolved oxygen concentration." According to the EPA, "the removal of ammonia in a wetland is dependent upon the configuration of the wetland and the availability of dissolved oxygen."

Bacteria, viruses, and other pathogens are removed through a combination of physical and chemical processes. Ultraviolet radiation from the sun and filtration into the sediment layers are physical factors. Chemically, exposure to biocides excreted by the plants and oxidation effectively kills off pathogens. The pathogens are also attacked and ultimately removed by parasitic worms or nematodes, as well as smaller organisms such as algae and fungi.

Dr. Seidel further commented on the use of plants in water purification systems and the lack of recognition of their effectiveness and importance in the scientific community:

> If you think about what is being done, in agriculture, in wastewater treatment, it is hard to maintain sanity. We showed in Krefield (Germany) that water pumped from the middle of the Rhine, passed through a simple filter and then poured through a field of these rushes could be put directly into water pipes without further treatment—pure drinking water. But men do not pursue these methods because they do not demand technology and thus make no profits. Nor do they want to do the plantings; they say they are engineers, not farmers.

Constructed Wetlands for Toxic Cleanup

The value of bulrushes, reeds, water hyacinths, and other wetland plants in cleaning up contaminated water and soil have been documented above. How are these "low tech" procedures being used today to stop the encroaching wave of toxicity? What has been done, and most importantly, what can you do to stem the tide of contamination upon the land, air, and water?

To date, numerous constructed wetlands across the world are being used to clean up industrial and agricultural waste. These are large wetlands built specifically to purify pollutants from industries such as textiles, petrochemicals, food processing, pulp and paper manufacturing, agricultural wastewater from fish, dairy and pig farms, and even highway runoff. These are large scale operations which typically use any of three types of constructed wetlands—free water surface; free floating with submerged plants; and subsurface flow wetlands.

The beauty of these natural systems is there are virtually no economies of scale that can keep the little guy out of the loop. These procedures can be done cost effectively for a small residential homeowner or business, as well as mega industrial sites. That is one reason for this book, to give all property owners/managers/stewards the wherewithal to solve problems in their own backyards—to efficiently and cost effectively clean up the land and water around them.

Free Water Surface Wetlands

These typically have between 20 and 30 centimeters of rooting soil, covered by approximately 20-40 centimeters of water. Dense emergent vegetation covers about 50% of the surface water. In North America, they may include the bulrush (Scirpus), cattail (Typha) or arrowhead (Latifolia). They root under the water line and grow to emerge above the water, thus the name emergent. The cleansing effect of these plants was described earlier.

Subsurface Flow Wetland

These are similar to free water surface wetlands but have a more porous bottom, comprised of gravel, sand, or soil. In these porous, aerated soil conditions, the wastewater is intended to filter down through the plant root structure where oxygen is abundant, thus enabling more nitrification. Sometimes combinations of wetland types are used to get better results. During cold winter months, for example, there is usually less oxygen available. This is caused in part by decomposing plants or animals that die-off in winter. The decomposition process uses oxygen and, therefore, makes it less available for nitrification and other procedures. To compensate for any lack of oxygen, some free water surface wetlands may be modified by constructing more porous bottoms to increase oxygen levels.

Free Floating and Submerged Wetlands

These wetlands have a combination of free floating non-rooted plants, and floating plants which are rooted in the bottom sediment. Free floating non-rooted plants include duckweed (Lemnoideae), water lettuce (Pistia stratiotes) and water hyacinths (Eichornia Crassipes), The most common rooted floating plants are water lilies (Nymphaeaceae), and lotus plants (Nelumbo nucifera).

More free floating plant benefits

These free floating lake, pond and wetland plants are typically in the crosshairs of so-called water management companies, many of whom believe the only good aquatic plant is a dead one. Duckweed in particular has been singled out as a nuisance that needs to be eradicated with herbicides. This is just one example of the short-sighted, arrogant and ignorant decision-making with regard to aquatic ecosystems. The many benefits of these tiny floating plants are not even considered, much less known about. They have somewhat similar water purification and oxygenation properties as those previously discussed, including the removal of heavy metals from the water.

Heavy metal pollution from industrial solid/liquid waste, sewage, etc. has turned many of our waterways into toxic dumpsites. The precipitous rise in Lead (Pb) and Cadmium (Cd) levels has been directly linked to long-lasting brain disorders, among other things. One would think it a priority to eliminate as much of these substances as possible. But that is not the case, as the prevalent use of herbicides has severely limited the ability of the natural world to purify the noxious mess that people create. These heavy metals can be substantially reduced, or even completely removed by doing practically nothing. That is to say, leave the duckweed and other aquatic plants alone, Put away your spray guns.

There have been many studies on the water purification properties of duckweed. One such study was conducted at Doon University in Uttarakhand, India on the potential of duckweed to remove lead (Pb) and cadmium (Cd) from waterways. Water samples with varying pH levels and heavy metal concentrations were used to reproduce conditions that may occur either in a natural environment. It concluded that optimum heavy metal removal was in water with pH levels ranging between 5 and 7. It was also found that heavy metal removal rose as water contamination levels increased (Figure 16 next page).

What also bears repeating is that Duckweed, and all other aquatic plants, bring higher levels of dissolved oxygen into the water via photosynthesis, and oxygen makes it possible for all other processes to function optimally.

Figure 17 Heavy Metal Removal Using Duckweed

Heavy Metal Concentrations/pH	% Removal
2mg/Liter at 9 pH	60.1
10mg/Liter at 7 pH	98.1
10mg/liter at 9 pH	41.6
2mg/Liter at 7 pH	84.8

Removal of Pharmaceuticals from Drainage Water with Duckweed

Reclaimed drainage water is commonly used for agricultural irrigation, especially in arid or semi-arid regions. However, this water is becoming increasingly contaminated with pharmaceutical waste, thus limiting its use for agriculture. A paper entitled "The Treatment of Drainage Water Containing Pharmaceuticals Using Duckweed (Lemme gibba)" was presented at the Conference on Technologies and Materials for Renewable Energy, Environment and Sustainability in Beirut - Lebanon. Data was compiled which showed the ability of free floating plants (in this case duckweed) to remove pharmaceutical waste from water.

Three pharmaceuticals typically found in water supplies are acetaminophen (ACT), diclofenac (DFC), and progesterone (PRG), which were the focus of the study. Figure 18 shows the capacity of free floating duckweed to remove pharmaceutical waste from water.

Figure 18 Pharmaceutical Waste Removal With Duckweed

Pharmaceutical	%Removal
Progesterone (PRG)	95.25
Diclofenac (DFC)	88.75
Acetaminophen (ACT)	84.51

Source: Energy Procedia Volume 74, August 2015

Practical Solutions Using Constructed Wetlands and Rain Gardens

Wetlands have many benefits, not only for water purification, but also flood control, aquifer replenishing, aesthetic beauty, wildlife habitat, and biodiversity. Constructing wetlands and/or raingardens presents a low tech, cost effective, and efficient way to solve water-related problems.

A good manager will customize wetland construction and use depending upon the specific situation. This may include levels and types of contaminants, zoning, topography, climate, flooding, and standing water after heavy rain. No two properties are alike, and there are no hard, across-the-board rules for solutions. This is where your creativity comes into play, and your ability to match the best custom marsh and/or raingarden designs to a specific property type.

Flooding and/or pools of standing water are usually deal breakers in real estate transactions. The FHA (Federal Housing Authority) will not guarantee mortgage loans on properties if, according to FHA Guidelines in Form HUD-92564-VC, "*grading does not provide positive drainage from structure,*" or with "*standing water proximate to structure.*" Water-related issues raise all kinds of red flags on most all property types—FHA or not.

I brokered a residential real estate acquisition (all cash), located in an Atlanta, GA, suburb. The buyers liked the property, except for the puddling that lasted sometimes several days after a heavy rain. The water was far enough from the building that seepage would not be a problem, nevertheless, airing on the side of caution, the buyers decided against the purchase. I asked them if the water issue was resolved would they go ahead with the transaction. They said yes, and I convinced them well-constructed raingardens would solve the problem, and that I would manage the construction.

I immediately went to work constructing two raingardens in the flooding areas. I followed standard protocol for sizing, based on impervious surface area, and dug two 12-inch areas, filled them with a mixture of compost, sand, and soil, and planted the appropriate plants.

After the next hard rain, puddling still occurred, although in much smaller amounts. Why? Because Georgia clay soil holds water almost as well as a porcelain cup. Did I do a percolation test on the soil prior to construction? Of course not, as I was in a hurry. The test would have indicated very poor absorption rates that require deeper gardens with more pervious soil. Solving the problem meant digging another foot deeper and filling with course sand and humus. This completely solved the water issues. They say knowledge is the short cut to experience. Well, I hope my experience provides you with this shortcut.

Lakefront Subdivisions

Lakefront subdivisions would do well to incorporate wetlands and raingardens into their association bylaws, if for no other reason than to put more money in the residents' pockets due to higher property values resulting from cleaner lakes. (The Lakes chapter explains the direct correlation between appraised real estate values and water clarity.)

If the buildings are on septic systems, seepage/overflow invariably occurs during heavy rainstorms. The results are usually devastating for lakes. Even with sewer lines installed, sewage overflow may still occur during heavy rains. Sewage seepage creates all kinds of problems, including toxic algae overgrowth, fish kills, water-born bacteria/viruses, etc.

Even if raw sewage does not overflow, excess stormwater runoff from the street most certainly will find its way into lower lying lakes, bringing with it grease, oil, pesticides, fertilizers, garbage, and who knows what.

A strategically placed wetland or large raingarden would catch, filter, and purify sewer and/or stormwater overflow. The wetland could be constructed along the banks of the lake at the overflow entry point(s). Other aquatic plants installed along the shoreline would provide additional purification. (See the Lakes sections for case studies on the effects aquatic vegetation has on water quality,)

A combination of wetlands and rain gardens could be even more effective. Raingardens could be built nearer to the source of runoff/overflow, possibly higher up and closer to the street or parking lot. This would diminish overflow at the lake. Also, raingardens can normally withstand both excessive drought and flooding, whereas wetlands require a semi-reliable source of water to keep them moist. A strategic combination of both can yield great dividends. It all depends on the location, topography, water flow, climate, pollution source(s), etc., to determine the best combination and type of "natural" sewer systems.

Commercial Solutions

Commercial properties with large impervious surfaces such as parking lots and roofs can put all that runoff to better, more profitable use. All or most of that water could be redirected to an on-site wetland, the size, depth, and configuration of which would be customized to the particular area's requirements. A property owner may ask, so why even bother? There are a number of reasons:

1) Fresh water is a valuable, necessary and, as of late, scarce resource (just ask any California resident or business owner). The property owner/manager can conserve this resource for irrigation or aquifer replenishing rather than let it flow into already overloaded sewer systems to be mixed with contaminants and eventually dumped into oceans, rivers, or bays.
2) Stormwater runoff expenses will be reduced
3) The wetland would create a park with wildlife habitat, and surrounding areas could also be used for employee recreation, picnics, or just a place to decompress from workplace stress.
4) Business owners will create goodwill among customers and local residents for protecting/purifying the local water supply.
5) Restaurants could grow their own vegetables and herbs on the well irrigated, fertile soil surrounding the wetland, and/or have an outdoor café overlooking the wildlife.
6) Sporting goods manufacturers and retailers (canoes, kayaks, scuba, fishing gear...) would be protecting the very resource that makes their businesses possible—clean water.
7) A boardwalk could be constructed over the wetland for walking/running trails

You could further capitalize on your wetland project in the fol lowing ways:

1) Invite universities or local water management authorities to study and document the wetland water quality compared to the water first entering into it.
2) Invite the press to cover said study and conduct an on-site interview.
3) Itemize the additional benefits in your marketing materials for selling or leasing the property, or for promoting your brand.
4) Start a positive domino effect. We live in a copy cat society. If all this favorable PR provides an edge, competitors will be sure to take notice and possibly follow suit.

Constructing a Marsh or Wetland

The first step is to analyze the entire area regarding amount and type of overflow—stormwater only, stormwater combined with sewage overflow, or any other type of contaminants. Highly contaminated water is best purified with plants like the bulrush, reeds, cattails, and arrowhead (See the earlier section of this chapter). Stormwater from the property alone would be much less toxic, enabling the use of a wider variety of plants.

Determine the primary source of overflow and locate the wetland in the water's path, but on the most level ground possible. In some cases, the water flow may have to be diverted using berms and swales. Look at the topography to see where stormwater naturally settles—this is where it should be, if possible. Check local restrictions for wetland proximity to buildings, septic systems, and wells. The size of the wetland is dependent upon runoff amounts and any other water sources leading into it

Excavate an area 1½ – 2 feet deep. If the area is always wet or has standing water most of the time, just fill the bottom with gravel and sand and cover it with at least 6 inches of mulch, soil, and humus. This is important for new root penetration. Initially, fairly constant water levels should be maintained so the roots are never exposed, and the leaves are not submerged at any time. After about six weeks of growth, the plants should be strong enough to withstand more fluctuating levels. The use of simple dykes and spillways can also help regulate water depth.

If you anticipate water being absent for long stretches, you could retain more water by lining the bottom with a plastic liner over a bed of fine sand to prevent stones from puncturing the plastic. If additional water is needed, the redirection of gray water from your house (shower and washing machine water can be easily piped to the marsh for purification and irrigation) and downspouts from the roof could significantly increase water supplies. You may not need the liner as the gray water and rain water may be enough to keep the marsh wet most of the time.

Marshes/wetlands are different than swamps, as the vegetation is mostly herbaceous as opposed to woody, and there is much more accumulation of peat on ground surfaces. Wetland plants are classified as herbaceous, having stems rather than woody trunks, and are also more commonly referred to as hydrophytes (plants partially or totally submerged in water). As previously mentioned, cattails, bulrushes, reeds, and canna lilies are a few of the most important wetland plants due to their water purifying capabilities. They adapt well to anaerobic (little to no oxygen) water due in part to their unique ability to pump oxygen from the leaves and stems down to the roots, and ultimately to the surrounding soil, creating oxygen-rich aerobic zones around each root. This creates aerobic microsites, which foster the growth of favorable bacteria and microbes, which further breaks down contaminants.

Types of Herbacious Plants

Emergent – rooted in the soil/sediment but with leaves, stems, and flowers above the water surface. These typically include rushes, arrowhead, and cattails.

Floating – may either be free floating or rooted in the soil and have leaves on the water surface with flowers and fruits above the surface. Water lily and duckweed are common floating plants.

Submergent – As the name implies, these grow completely below the water's surface and include eelgrass, wild celery, and coontail.

Chapter Six

Living Lakes

Transforming Dead Lakes into Healthy Ecosystems

> A lake is the landscape's most beautiful and expressive feature. It is the earth's eye, looking into which the beholder measures the depth of his own nature.
> – Henry David thorough

Lakes are living, breathing beings. They are not static, inert bodies of water to be artificially manipulated and altered. They are complex, diverse ecosystems with dynamic, symbiotic relationships in constant interaction and with ever-changing biological, chemical and physical cycles.

Lakes are intelligent and alive and should be dealt with as such. They are self-regulating systems that maintain a state of equilibrium—a balance of plants, organisms, animals, and biological compounds. which usually compensate for the onslaught of man-made pollution.

Many lake management practices today do not fully utilize this synergy and work against the innate wisdom of lake ecosystems. Symptoms such as weed overgrowth are dealt with as single, unrelated problems that are temporarily solved with the application of herbicides. There is normally no discussion about eliminating the ultimate source of the problem(s) and/or using a whole-systems approach to solving it.

Herbicide applications eliminate weed overgrowth (for a while) but are damaging to the balance of the system and its ability to self-regulate. For every action, there is an equal and opposite reaction, the true consequences of which are seldom thought of much less physically dealt with. This is great for the herbicide companies, as treatment will be required ad infinitum.

Indiscriminately dredging bottoms of lakes to remove weeds is another narrow, limiting procedure. The importance of these submerged macrophytes (weeds) to the overall health of the lake and water clarity will be discussed later.

As with all else in the natural world, lakes are cyclical in nature, with a constant flow of energy and matter. Disrupting enough of these flows would be like cutting an artery in your body. Lakes have open ended energy flows, in that there is a continuous inflow of new energy in the form of sunlight, which then initiates photosynthesis with the aquatic plants and algae. This creates oxygen, which is consumed by aquatic life, from large fish down to the smallest of micro organisms. These organisms initiate an array of bio-chemical processes, one being the decomposition of dead matter.

A full understanding of lake dynamics enables one to work with those forces and complement them to recreate balance. This is far less expensive in the long run, more efficient, inflicts no other damage, and is more often than not a permanent solution.

The water quality of lakes in the U.S. is abysmal at best. Many have undergone major transformation—from crystal clear lakes with supportive vegetation and abundant aquatic life, to dirty water choked with algae and contaminated with pesticide and fertilizer runoff, as well as bacteria, oil, and chemicals from stormwater overflow, sewer drainage, and septic tank seepage. In addition, most if not all of the native aquatic plants are typically removed for "aesthetic" purposes and replaced by lawns which run right up to the water line. It's no wonder the lakes are either dead or dying, resulting in major health and financial cost.

The Financial Case for Healthy Lakes

Why place so much emphasis on clear, balanced lakes? One of many reasons is dirty lakes are tantamount to throwing away large sums of money, not to mention adverse health effects, loss of business, etc.

In the following example, there was a $560 million property value loss for 37 lake properties in Minnesota based on water clarity alone, and there are many other studies that demonstrate the direct effect water clarity has on lake community property values.

A study by the Mississippi Headwaters Board and Bemidji State University quantified the financial gain or loss as related to lake water clarity. Hedonic regression analysis was used to isolate water clarity as it affects fair market value. To do this, the many variables that alter sales price had to be adjusted in order to single out the value of water clarity. The 37 lakes were divided into 6 groups, each with different location characteristics. Formulas were used on each group to negate any location differences.

There was a direct correlation between price and environmental quality. Properties with high quality commanded higher market prices. The properties were also adjusted to account for those environmental differences. There were three categories of environmental quality:

1) High – had a large buffer zone between buildings, lawns, driveways, etc. and the lakefront. There was emergent aquatic vegetation along the littoral zone (shallow areas near the shore line).
2) Typical – had a thin buffer zone relative to the high quality scenario. Boat lifts and docks used up large areas of the lakefront.
3) Poor – grass extended right up to the water's edge, with no aquatic vegetation present.

Most of the lake frontage was either developed, or ready to be

Figure 19

Water clarity as it affects property values on 37 Minnesota lakes.

Lake	Mean Clarity (meters)	Price change/FF for 1 meter Increase	Price change/FF for 1 meter Decrease	Total FF	Total change in property prices for 1 meter Increase	Total change in property prices for 1 meter Decrease
Big Sandy	1.38	$218.00	-$516.23	324,057	$63,579,983	-$150,560,122
Dam	3.56	6.32	-8.41	19,196	109,104	-145,347
Esquagamah	1.39	17.60	-41.26	28,313	448,369	-1,051,391
Farm Island	4.22	24.95	-31.72	63,660	1,429,485	-1,817,365
Ross	1.43	12.29	-27.87	26,575	294,062	-666,581
Spirit	4.28	7.01	-8.89	24,390	153,846	-195,099
Alexander	4.89	8.99	-11.06	78,055	631,660	-776,842
Bay	4.14	10.46	-13.36	106,969	1,006,845	-1,286,636
Fish Trap	3.74	5.55	-7.29	57,319	206,117	-375,917
Gulf	3.42	39.23	-52.91	185,179	6,538,349	-8,817,887
Norway	2.83	3.36	-4.85	19,433	58,829	-84,864
Pelican	4.95	30.37	-37.25	115,165	3,147,922	-3,860,639
Platte	2.01	6.48	-11.05	57,652	336,493	-573,580
Roosevelt	3.88	38.80	-50.42	82,052	2,865,342	-3,724,297
Shamineau	5.11	6.69	-8.16	49,413	297,500	-362,930
Upper Hay	2.62	3.40	-5.06	18,232	55,820	-83,117
Balsam	3.6	1.08	-1.43	6,500	35,478	-46,975
Pokegama	4.9	29.53	-36.29	184,460	4,902,393	-6,024,648
Prairie	1.79	4.20	-7.75	64,774	244,845	-451,798
Wabana	4.7	3.73	-4.62	104,751	351,649	-435,554
Ada	4.34	3.14	-3.97	8,117	79,458	-100,462
Kabekona	3.86	6.00	-7.82	48,238	260,485	-339,499
Leech	3.04	423.58	-594.16	882,248	93,425,651	-131,049,117
Ten Mile	6.61	9.32	-10.85	108,720	911,943	-1,061,650
Woman	4.12	13.59	-17.39	144,781	1,770,816	-2,265,967
4th Crowing	2.8	15.84	-22.92	20,725	295,455	-427515
8th Crowing	2.76	18.73	-27.26	23,900	402,882	-586632
Belle Taine	6.38	28.91	-33.85	108,594	2,825,507	-3,308,315
Fish hook	3.36	61.02	-82.75	34,282	1,882,698	-2,553,152
George	2.71	26.60	-38.99	26,550	635,607	-931,666

	Mean Clarity	Price change/FF for 1 meter		Total FF	Total change in property prices for 1 meter	
Lake	(meters)	Increase	Decrease		Increase	Decrease
Long	5.8	2.26	-2.69	14,979	30,467	-36,264
Benidji	2.85	193.48	-278.00	69,399	10,070,488	-14,469,691
Cass	4.02	326.36	-420.20	195,396	15,942,278	-20,526,244
Irving	1.51	34.02	-72.67	21,966	672,555	-1,436,642
Marquette	3.01	9.97	-14.03	21,384	191,878	-270,015
Big Turtle	3	20.70	-29.17	53,394	994,730	-1,401,752
Big Wolf	3.13	17.16	-23.83	35,511	548,431	-761,604

Total Price Changes:

Total property appreciation for a 1 meter increase in water clarity: $217.635,420

Total property devaluation for a 1 meter decrease in water clarity: $362,867,777$

developed (vacant lot in a neighborhood). All lakefront properties were residential with similar construction and zoning. Construction was further broken down by gross living area, age, number of bathrooms, and HVAC system. Land prices were obtained from the local county tax assessors office. The Minnesota Pollution Control Agency supplied the water quality information.

The study showed that the combined property values on 37 lakes in Minnesota increased over $217 million for just a one-meter increase in water clarity. Conversely, a one-meter decrease in water clarity devalued the combined properties over $360 million. **That's over a $577 million turnaround in property value if measures were taken to improve water clarity rather than letting visibility degrade by 1 meter**.

The price change per lake front foot (FF) was also documented.

The mean price increase was $45.64 per lake front foot for a one-meter increase in water clarity. Multiply this times the total front feet (3,434,329) and you get a $154,544,805 net property increase. If you consider the decrease in values ($69.36 mean decrease/FF) from a decrease in water clarity, the net decrease in value per FF is $238,205,059, for a total turnaround of $392,749,864 based on the average lake front foot. Bear in mind, these values could easily be doubled in todays inflated real estate market and devalued dollar.

Another study in Saltworks Creek inlet along the Severn River northwest of Annapolis, Maryland, calculated the effects of fecal coliform counts on property values. Forty-one residential properties along the upper reaches of the inlet were studied. Coliform counts around the inlet were much higher than along the Severn River—increasing from approximately 50 counts per 100 ml at the mouth to 135 counts per 100 ml about a half mile into the inlet, and about 240 counts per 100 ml about one mile from the mouth. By factoring out other variables and isolating water quality as it related to property values, the projected increase in value was approximately a combined $230,000 based on a hypothetical reduction in fecal coliform. This represented a 2 % increase in value for the 41 properties based on fecal coliform reduction alone. (Leggett et al 1999)

The total economic impact of clean water is huge when viewing the whole picture, not just net property value increases as shown above. This includes:

1) Additional tax revenue for municipalities from increased property values.
2) Lower healthcare costs due to reduced exposure to contaminated water, cyanotoxins, etc. (These costs are itemized in more detail later.)
3) Lower lake-maintenance costs. Clean lakes eliminate the need for herbicides and mechanical removal of weed overgrowth According to the Ohio EPA, algae overgrowth treat-

ment alone can exceed $200,000 per month, per water system in Ohio

4) More business for sporting goods or similar companies selling such items such as fishing gear, snorkeling equipment (you can't see anything in dirty water), canoes, rafts, scuba gear, and the like.
5) Increased Tourism. Many lakes have public beach areas. Clear, healthy lakes will increase tourism exponentially, and the money they spend all goes right into the local economy.
6) More disposable income for lakefront property owners due to increased equity from rising property values.

These are just a few of the quantifiable benefits, not to mention protecting the drinking water supply, creating better fish and wildlife habitat, maintaining a deep respect for the land, and providing the next generation with a better quality of life.

We did a Google search for "lakes so clear you can see fish swimming." Beaver Lake came up number one on Google's first page and had 230 reviews. Other listings on Google's first page were: best retreats, best swimming, and best fishing lakes, all with many good reviews. What do you think this positive exposure would do to a lake's local economy? Would it be worth it to take the necessary steps to rebalance the lake ecosystem? Property value increases alone make it worth the time and expense, then factor everything else, as mentioned above, and look at the bottom line. This is not to mention what you will leave behind for your children's children. To quote Thomas Jefferson again: *"No man can by natural right oblige the lands he occupied, or the persons who succeeded him in that occupation, to the payment of debts contracted by him. For if he could, he might during his own life eat up the usufruct of the lands for several generations to come, and then the lands would belong to the dead, and not the living."*

Health Effects of Dirty Lakes

One harmful by-product of lakes contaminated with excessive amounts of nutrients from fertilizer runoff and sewage overflow is algae. Some algae contains cyanobacteria, and produces cyanotoxins, which are toxic to the liver and kidneys, and cause upper respiratory disease and a host of other problems to humans and animals alike.

The state of Oklahoma limits public exposure to freshwater algae as it is considered a severe health threat. It requires agencies monitoring recreational lakes to post algae concentrations for the public to see. If algae cell counts exceed 100,000 cells per milliliter, people are warned not to go near the water.

In 2010, the Ohio EPA sampled water in Lake Erie and other inland lakes as part of their Inland Lake Monitoring Program. The amount of cyanotoxins found in these samples were:

79 random samples – over 20 micrograms (µg) /liter

Grand Lake St. Mary's – over 2,000 micrograms (µg) /liter

Lake Erie – over 570 micrograms (µg) /liter This is 25 times more cyanotoxins than the World Health Organization's tolerance for recreational waterways.

[1 microgram (µg) in mass equals: 0.000001 grams (g)]

Another species of algae known as golden algae was first monitored in North America in the 1980s. This invasive species is more known for massive fish kills and is found mostly in the southern United States. It has a harmful effect on zooplankton, which is the primary food source for most freshwater fish. Zooplankton provide many other vital roles in the overall health of lakes and will be discussed later. Although the adverse health effects of golden algae on people has not been conclusively documented, the primary source of this algae overgrowth is the same as blue-green algae, that being high concentrations of nutrients from external, man-made sources.

Aside from health problems and fish kills, algae overgrowth has a devastating effect on aquatic plants, which play an integral role in maintaining the balance of the lake ecosystems. Out-of-control algae blooms attach to the leaves of submerged plants, limiting their growth, or killing the plant outright. Dense algae blooms covering the surface water also block out sunlight, which further inhibits aquatic plant growth, thus impeding oxygen production. This is known as eutrophication, or the increased trophic conditions of a lake. The number one cause of eutrophication is an overabundance of organic nutrients—more specifically, phosphorus. This phosphorus overload is the direct result of sewage and wastewater runoff, sewage being the primary culprit as it contains high levels of detergent (phosphates) and fecal phosphorus.

Naturally occurring aquatic plants are able to neutralize much of this pollution when given the chance, as they are self-regulating, self-purifying, and maintain a healthy biological balance.

Lake Ecosystems

Lakes are living,-breathing organisms with symbiotic relationships somewhat similar to the human body. A good lake manager understands these systems and works **with** them to optimize health and performance.

Lakes have different zones or subsystems all working within the larger context of the whole lake ecosystem. Sunlight is the primary energy source for lakes. Two zones were created to categorize the effects of sunlight, or lack thereof. These are:

Trophogenic Zone – lighted areas with sunlight penetration of surface and medium depth water. Photosynthesis occurs in this zone, which produces oxygen and releases organic compounds.

Tropholytic Zone – deeper, darker areas with minimal to no sunlight penetration.

Other lake zones include:

1) **Pelagic Zone** – These are the open-water, middle areas of a lake with the most currents and turbulence.
2) **Littoral Zone** – This covers the shallow edges of the lake. There is plenty of sunlight penetration here, and as such, it is also part of the Trophogenic zone. This zone captures most of the sediments, chemicals, nutrients, and other pollutants entering the lake. Vegetation here includes both emergent (rooted in bottom sediment and extending above the water line) and submerged aquatic plants (macrophytes). These plants typically remove most or all of the contaminants before reaching the open areas of the lake. The plants in this zone are extremely important to lake water quality, and also provide breeding grounds and cover for fish, amphibians, and other animals.

Figure 20 Vegetated littoral zone, and open pelagic zones of a large freshwater lake

1) **Profundal Zone** – This zone is at the lake bottom with little or no light. Due to the lack of light, it is part of the Tropholytic zone. No photosynthesis occurs here. Bacteria and fungi decompose organic matter that has sunk to the lake bottom. Oxygen is consumed in this process, resulting in anaerobic (lacking oxygen) conditions at lake bottoms.

Other zones related to temperature and depth are the epilimnion, which includes the upper, warmer waters, and the hypolimnion, or lower, colder waters.

Living Communities Within the Zones

Open-Water Pelagic Zone Communities

Plankton and free swimming aquatic animals independent of currents (mostly fish), live predominately in this zone. Plankton is a community of organisms suspended in water, consisting of phytoplankton and zooplankton. Some plankton have weak propulsion mechanisms while others are totally dependent on the currents for mobility. Plankton are broken down into two main groups:

Phytoplankton – consist of blue-green algae, and diatoms (minute unicellular algae with silica shells). Chlorophyll-containing phytoplankton creates oxygen from photosynthesis using sunlight as an energy source. Some Phytoplankton contain cyanobacteria, which is toxic to humans, animals, and other lake organisms such as zooplankton (discussed below). If completely out of control, it will choke the lake and kill the biological systems.

Zooplankton live here as well, and help regulate the algae population, as algae is a primary food source for some zooplankton. The absence or presence of zooplankton is a primary factor in lake water quality/clarity. The various trophic levels (position in the food chain) of zooplankton include herbivores (plant eaters), bacteriavores (bacteria eaters), and zooplanktivores (feeding on other smaller zooplankton). Some are omnivores, meaning they feed on zooplankton, plants, and bacteria alike. The majority of zooplankton feed on phytoplankton. Since some phytoplankton contain algae and bacteria, this predator/prey relationship prevents phytoplankton/algae overgrowth, resulting in clearer, healthier, more balanced lakes. There are three major classes of zooplankton found in freshwater lakes:

1) **Protozoans** – tiny unicellular organisms that eat primarily bacteria and some forms of algae. These include flagellates, which have hair-like cilia on their surface, helping propel them through the water; and ciliates, which can be found as both an amoeba and swimming flagellate.
2) **Rotifers** – somewhat larger, multi-cellular organisms (from 30 micrometers to 1 millimeter in length). They are distinguishable by two lobes surrounded by cilia (figure 21), which appear to rotate and resemble two turning wheels. These beating cilia create water currents—a sort of vortex that helps capture food. The name rotifer is derived from the Latin rota, or wheel. They eat algae, protozoa (such as amoeba and paramecium), and small bits of plant or animal matter floating in the current.
3) **Crustaceans** – These are filter feeders characterized by their hard external skeletons and antennae (figure 22). The most common zooplankton crustaceans are copepods and cladocerans, and are anywhere between 100 micrometers and 1 millimeter in length. Both copepods and cladocerans (commonly called water fleas, or Daphnia) are omnivorous, normally eating approximately 70% phytoplankton and 30% protozoans. The fine feeding filters enable them to eat large bacteria as well.

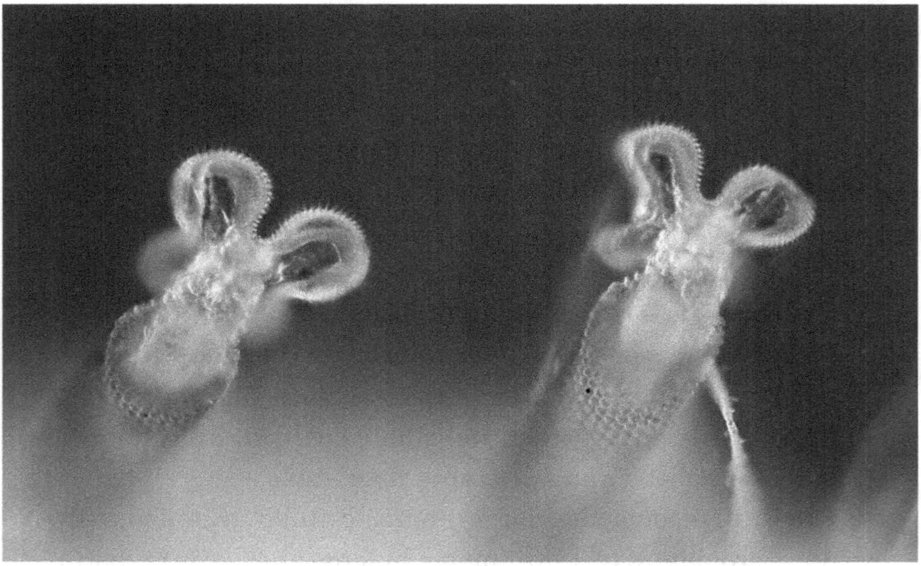

Figure 21 Close-up up shot of freshwater zooplankton rotifers

Figure 22 Close-up shot of freshwater zoopolankton crustacean

Evidence shows that when the feeding rates of zooplankton exceeds phytoplankton production, clearer lakes result. However, some cyanobacteria is toxic to zooplankton and either kills or inhibits their growth. When this type of cyanobacteria predominates, the balance may be upset and could create out of control algae blooms.

The Benthos Community

This community lives in and around the bottom sediment of lakes. The diversity of the community living in this region is largely dependent upon the bottom sediment composition: epipelic organisms live on/in mud; episammic live on/in sand; and epiphytic organisms attach themselves to submerged plants or rocks and eat (graze) on the algae attached to those surfaces. These include snails, also referred to as "scrapers." Also exclusive to this community are detrivorous animals that feed on dead organic matter. They are also known as shredders as these organisms break down, or shred dead matter such as leaves into finer particles. Amphipods and isopods are the most common bottom feeding shredders.

The benthic zone is broken down into two categories: 1) the deepest areas of the lake bottom in the profundal zone, and 2) the bottom of the shallower areas of the littoral zone. The deeper, darker areas are comprised of organisms that consume or decompose organic matter that settled to the bottom. The size of these organisms is directly related to the amount and quality of organic matter available there. Since most of the organic matter is partially decomposed before reaching the lake bottom, it has relatively low nutritional value.

It's All Connected

Lake communities are by no means exclusive of each other. On the contrary, they are interrelated and mutually dependent. This is indicative of lake ecosystems as a whole. The creation of various zones and categories is used to clarify the workings of a larger intricate web of co-dependent, cause-effect relationships. Like everything else in the natural world, there are no clear boundaries. For example: benthos organisms are dependent upon zooplankton of the pelagic zone, in that partially digested algae in the heavier zooplankton feces sinks to the bottom where it is eaten by benthos organisms. Phytoplankton from the pelagic zone is carried to the littoral zone by currents. There it is trapped by the littoral zone plants and provides a food source for the filter feeders such as mussels, that live there.

As previously discussed, algae/cyanobacteria overgrowth is a major health concern—for humans, animals, and lake biosystems. Maintaining a balance of zooplankton and phytoplankton is just one cause-effect relationship that is critical to preventing this problem. The presence or absence of aquatic plants and the various other cycles—carbon, phosphorus, etc.—all play a role as well.

Cycles

Not unlike the human body, lakes have biological and respiratory cycles, which maintain balance and overall health. Viewing lakes in this light, as opposed to an inert hole in the ground filled with water, will reveal a host of synergistic, problem-solving opportunities.

The Carbon Cycle

Carbon found in lakes is classified into three categories: Dissolved Inorganic Carbon (DIC), which includes carbon dioxide; Dissolved Organic Carbon (DOC); and Particulate Organic Carbon (POC). DOC is produced by organism excretions, microbial decomposition of dead organisms, and cell breakdown. DOC is an important energy and carbon source for aquatic bacteria. As such, the bacteria maintain balance by consuming DOC and help prevent DOC overloads.

The largest input of dissolved inorganic carbon (DIC) into lakes is from atmospheric carbon dioxide. Lake surface water literally breathes in carbon dioxide directly from the atmosphere. This respiration increases with water turbulence. The more wave action, the more carbon dioxide is absorbed. The lake then extracts (inhales) the carbon dioxide during the photosynthesis activity of the aquatic plants, and exhales oxygen back into the water and air.

Particulate Organic Carbon (POC) is found in organisms and detritus such as leaf litter and dead organisms. POC typically settles in the bottom sediment where it is consumed by bottom-feeding organisms and can be transformed into DOC through their excretion and secretion.

Nitrogen Cycle

Nitrogen is the most prevalent gas in the atmosphere, and diffuses into water bodies as dissolved elemental Nitrogen (N_2). However, it is largely inaccessible to plant and animal life in this state. It first needs to be "fixed," or converted into more usable forms. Microscopic organisms produce the enzyme nitrogenase, which, through series of microbial transformations, converts nitrogen into ammonia. Total ammonia exists in two chemical forms, ammonia, which is toxic to fish and plant life, and non-toxic ammonium. Whether ammonia or ammonium predominates as the end result of this process depends upon the pH levels of the water body. A relatively low pH creates an environment conducive to non-toxic ammonium, while very high pH levels favor ammonia.

The rules of thumb are: ammonium predominates almost exclusively with pH levels below 8, while ammonia is most abundant with pH levels above 10.5. A typical water body with a pH of 8, for example, is comprised of about 10% ammonia, and 90% ammonium. The ammonium/ammonia balance favors ammonium in healthy lakes.

Total ammonia (in either form) is then further transformed through the process of nitrification, which converts it to useable forms for plants and animals. Here, ammonia oxidizing bacteria, Nitrosomonas, convert ammonia to nitrite, after which nitrite oxidizing bacteria, Nitrobacter, convert nitrite to nitrate. These bacteria are ubiquitous in aerobic (oxygen rich) environments, and these chemical processes all require the presence of oxygen.

These forms of "fixed" nitrogen compounds are an important food source for phytoplankton, including algae. Aquatic plants, however, can use only nitrate and ammonium as a food source. Therefore, it is important that the complete nitrification process takes place to maintain healthy plant life.

Cause-effect relationships

Many so-called lake managers seem to be operating in a bubble, with no thought or consideration given to the biological balance and chemical processes that take place. A deeper understanding would reveal simple, cost-effective solutions for dead or dying lakes.

For example, if a lake is overgrown with algae the typical response would be to spray herbicides on the lake in order to kill the algae. Well, this sets off a chain of events that only exacerbate the problem.

1) Spraying herbicides kills not only algae, but also free floating plants such as duckweed and lily pads, as well as some submerged plants. Bacteria then decompose these dead plants and organisms. This process uses a lot of oxygen, resulting in oxygen-starved lakes.
2) This lack of oxygen sets off other processes such as fish kills. When those fish die from lack of oxygen, the decomposition of their bodies consumes even more oxygen resulting in additional oxygen-depleted dead zones.
3) The nitrogen fixing and nitrification processes which convert elemental nitrogen into ammonia/ammonium, nitrites and then nitrates require aerobic, oxygen-rich water. Lack of oxygen severely limits the ability of ammonia and nitrite oxidizing bacteria to complete these processes.
4) Little or no ammonia and nitrite oxidation would create a preponderance of toxic ammonia and insufficient nitrates for

aquatic plant intake.

5) These diminished biological processes make lakes even more susceptible to contamination from fertilizer and agricultural run-off.

Phosphorus Cycle

Naturally occurring phosphorus is limited in most lakes, unlike carbon and nitrogen, which are consistently entering the water through contact with the atmosphere. Phosphorus naturally enters lakes via animal secretions and decomposition processes. It then sinks to the bottom where it is absorbed by the sediment. This is where the highest concentrations of phosphorus are normally found. The phosphorus is literally trapped there if the sediment surface contains high levels of oxygen. Oxygen helps create the compound ferric iron oxide (FEOOH), which has a high phosphorus absorption capacity, and thus prevents phosphorus from entering the main water body.

Aquatic plants rooted in lake bottoms use phosphorus as a nutrient for normal growth. Phytoplankton absorb the phosphorus as well, which leads to relatively low levels in healthy lakes. The balance between phosphorus and nitrogen almost always favors nitrogen in healthy, clear lakes.

Phosphorus levels are **artificially increased** through wastewater runoff, high phosphorus detergents, fertilizers, and watershed erosion. Abnormally **high phosphorus levels** create a domino effect of problems:

1) Submerged aquatic plants obtain nutrients from bottom sediment, and if the sediment is too high in phosphorus, the plants' uptake of phosphorus is abnormally high as well. As levels increase, the plants become overgrown with algae which restricts growth or even kills the plants.
2) Compromised aquatic plants with limited photosynthetic activity results in reduced oxygen levels in the immediate zone.

3) Phosphorus is easily released from the oxygen-starved (anoxic) conditions in and around the sediment. This is called internal phosphorus loading, which accelerates the release of phosphorus back into the upper water body. The release of phosphorus from the sediment back into the water is also caused by wind and water turbulence.
4) Increased phosphorus levels in the water accelerate algae blooms, which further deprive the lake of oxygen while blocking out valuable sunlight for the aquatic plants.
5) Fish kills occur from lack of oxygen
6) Fish populations are further depleted as they cannot reproduce due to the oxygen-starved conditions on the sediment surface.

These and other cause-effect relationships create a snowballing effect that can easily get out of control.

Aquatic Plants

Aquatic plants play a major role in balancing, cleansing, and regenerating lake ecosystems. Lake aquatic plants are classified into three groups: Submerged, Emergent, and Floating.

Submerged Macrophytes

These underwater rooted plants require light and are, therefore, located closer to the edges of deep lakes where the water is shallower and light penetration is favorable to their growth. They grow throughout the entire lake bottom in shallower lakes. These plants are vital to lake ecosystems as they:

1) Provide habitat and cover for fish breeding
2) Remove nitrogen, phosphorus, and other nutrients from the water and sediment
3) Create more oxygen in the water and sediment
4) Help reduce suspended sediment by restricting water currents

5) Inhibit algae growth

Algae growth is minimized from a few different angles. First, these plants compete with algae for food, as they both consume nutrients such as phosphorus and nitrogen. Second, the plants create more oxygen in the sediment as well as the surrounding water. Increased oxygen levels in the sediment literally traps nutrients like phosphorus that settled there and prevents it from assimilating back into the water.

If there were little to no oxygen present in the area, the phosphorus would release back into the water. As additional phosphorus is re -suspended, this food source would stimulatee algae growth and creates a snowball effect. In more scientific terms, this is called galloping eutrophication, or self-accelerating eutrophication.

Third, some submerged plant species release anti-algal compounds into the water, which suppresses or kills the algae blooms. Ceratophyllum demersum (also known as Coontail) is a non-rooting submerged plant that has been shown to release algaecides composed of sulfur compounds. These help inhibit cyanobacteria-containing phytoplankton.

Several different studies showed the Myriophyllum family releasing compounds which target algae and cyanobacteria. Myriophyllum spicatum is one submerged aquatic plant species with anti-algal activity, most notably the release of acidic phenolic compounds. It is an invasive, non-native plant, so using it for lake management in the U.S. would not be recommended. There are many other alleopathic macrophytes, the descriptions of which are beyond the scope of this book.

Submerged plants, such as eel grass (Valisneria Americana), also known as tapegrass or water celery, are frequently used for water restoration. They are hardy plants able to withstand strong water currents and limited sunlight penetration. They provide excellent cover and breeding grounds for bass, reduce sediment turbidity, and provide oxygen to the lake bottom.

Emergent Macrophytes

These plants are rooted under water and grow above the water's surface. They are located along the shallow edges of lakes (littoral zone) and are most noted for their exceptional water purifying qualities. Some species include:

Bulrush (Scirpus Validas)

This species is the most efficient at nitrogen removal. It is used extensively as a major part of wastewater treatment processes. See the Constructed Wetlands section of the Water Management chapter for more on the purifying qualities of the bulrush. It grows relatively slowly, making it unlikely to overgrow and take over a lake ecosystem.

Reeds (Phragmites Communis)

These are second only to the bulrush in their ability to remove nitrogen from the water and sediment

Cattails (Typha Latifala)

Cattails are the least efficient at nitrogen and phosphorus removal as compared to the bulrush and reeds. They also have a tendency to die out if overloaded with nutrients or contaminants. One should exercise caution with the cattail as it reproduces aggressively, and can easily take over the littoral zone of a lake—essentially crowding out other species. The county of Pinellas, Florida, wetland management and mosquito control unit actually went to great lengths to eradicate the cattails from many different wetland sites. They are now in the process of planting bulrushes, water lilies, eel grass, and cypress in their place.

Pickerel Weed (Pontederia Cordata

These plants are also effective at removing excess nutrients and other contaminants.

Floating-Leaved Macrophytes

As the name implies, the leaves of these plants float on the water's surface, and are classified as either rooted in the bottom sediment or free floating. The rooted species obtain most or all of their nutrients directly from the sediment. Free-floating plants get all their nutrients directly from the water. This creates food competition with the algae. These floating-leaved plants are typically broad-leafed and, as such, block out considerable areas of sunlight. Relative lack of sunlight and lower nutrient levels has a direct, adverse effect on phytoplankton and can reduce algae counts significantly. These macrophytes grow predominately in still water and are therefore found mostly around lake edges and in more wind protected areas such as coves or inlets.

The rooted species include waterlily (Naphar variegatum) and pondweed (Potamogetum). The pondweed is the most dominant floating-leaved plant in the Marsh Lake study below. The free-floating species includes duckweed (Lemma minor) and bladderwort (Utricularia vulgaris).

Restoration of Marsh Lake

Marsh Lake is an impounded (man-made) lake in Minnesota. There was a rapid decline in water quality after impoundment due to murky water from sediment suspension, aquatic plant loss, and invasive species.

Prior to impoundment, this area was a low flood plain with frequent changes in water levels—from high-level flooding, to dry, de-watered periods. After impoundment, dams were constructed in order to maintain a constant water level. This unchanging level disrupted the natural rhythms and cycles of the lake. Most lakes go through periods of drought and extended rainy seasons, which leads to large fluctuations in water levels. The abnormally constant levels resulting from the dams came at the expense of the aquatic plants.

Under normal conditions, plants are able to germinate in the mudflats created by low water levels. These mudflats are nutrient-rich from decomposed organic matter, providing fertile ground for macrophyte growth. This whole process requires dewatered dry periods, which expose once submerged areas to air and sunlight.

Marsh Lake went through a period of severe drought from 1988 to 1989. The dam could not prevent a significant drop in water level. This enabled emergent aquatic plants to take root in the exposed, dewatered areas. The result: In 1991, there were 1,574 acres of emergent aquatic plants in the littoral zone of Marsh Lake. In 1998, after some 7 years of stable high water levels artificially maintained by dams, the emergent macrophyte population was reduced to 1,032 acres.

This is significant because it created a whole chain of events which eroded lake water quality.

1) Nutrient uptake was diminished, enabling the formation of toxic algae blooms. The overgrown algae attached to remaining plants and inhibited their growth. Suspended algae reduced water clarity, thus limiting sunlight penetration, which further inhibited submerged plant growth.
2) Reduced plant oxygen production resulted in more anaerobic zones in the sediment and water. This enabled the release of phosphorus from the sediment back into the water, which also contributed to nutrient overload. Reduced oxygen levels adversely affect fish and the rest of the food chain all the way down to zooplankton. As mentioned earlier, zooplankton consume algae, therefore, helping to check overgrowth and maintain balance. Reduced oxygen levels alone can adversely affect the whole lake ecology resulting in galloping eutrophication.
3) Loss of submerged plants increased water currents and turbidity. This created more suspended sediment which diminished water clarity and lowered light penetration.
4) Native fish populations such as the northern pike were dras-

tically reduced due to diminished spawning grounds from submerged aquatic plant loss. These fish preyed on the zooplankton-eating carp and kept them under control. The carp populations increased at the expense of vital zooplankton.

Reasons for Plant Loss in Marsh Lake

1) Reduced light penetration from suspended sediment inhibited plant growth.
2) Grazing by high carp fish populations. Carp eat plankton and algae feeders such as zooplankton. This creates an imbalance between algae and zooplankton, leading to algae blooms which kill or inhibit aquatic plant growth
3) Lower zooplankton populations limited this important food source for young native fish, such as pike, which would normally feed on carp. Lower pike populations resulted in an overabundance of carp.
4) Constant water levels prevented mudflat exposure, which impeded seed germination

Solutions

1) Periodically lower lake levels to reestablish aquatic vegetation, which creates a chain of lake restoration events.
2) Create a fishway near the dam to enable upstream fish migration, thus enhancing and diversifying the fish population. This is a waterway of pebbles and boulders (to slow downward water flow) leading up to the lake from the stream below.
3) Curtail nutrient loading and other contaminants from nearby farms, subdivisions, etc.

Lake Washington (WA)

In the early 1960's, Lake Washington (in Washington state) was a eutrophic lake with overgrown algae blooms and only one meter of water clarity. The primary cause of this poor condition was typical for lakes around the world—urbanization of the watershed surrounding lakes. This buildup depleted wetlands, resulting in less water purification capabilities and more sewage and industrial discharge from homes, businesses, roads, etc.

Steps were taken to restore the lake to its original condition, which included installing a new sewage pipeline. This procedure alone accounted for a steep drop in phosphorus levels to an optimal level, or equilibrium, resulting in a three-meter increase in water clarity.

Additional steps included the physical removal of zooplankton predators (zooplanktivorous fish) such as carp. This created another series of interrelated events.

1) The zooplankton population increase resulted in more phytoplankton and algae consumption.
2) Reduced suspended algae levels enabled more sunlight penetration, which stimulated more submerged plant growth.
3) Additional plant growth created other chains of events, including:
    a. More oxygen production in the water and sediment, which represses phosphorus integration into the water from the sediment and supports healthy populations of fish, amphibians, etc.
    b. Lower water currents, which prevent stirred-up sediment from clouding the water, enable more sunlight penetration for submerged plant growth.
    c. New breeding areas for native fish.

A recent article in the Journal of Limnology stated that *"freshwater macrophytes are one of the fundamental factors that influence the structure of freshwater ecosystems ... structurally complex habitats provide an increased availability of riches for resident animals ... results in increased species diversity."*

The practice of indiscriminate herbicide application to kill "weeds" is self-destructive. This practice is outdated and counterproductive, given all the scientific literature and case studies that prove the value of aquatic plants.

The Florida Fish and Wildlife commission maintains that fish and wildlife populations are healthiest when submerged aquatic vegetation is present. One of their lake restoration projects involved planting eel grass to restore Lake Jesup in Florida. One of the many benefits was the creation of more suitable habitat for bass and other fish to breed.

Lake Zwemlust (The Netherlands)

This shallow Dutch lake was in an advanced eutrophic state—overgrown with algae blooms and cyanobacteria. Steps taken to solve the problem started with draining the lake and to remove all the fish. When the lake filled up again, there were still high levels of nutrients due to external pollution sources that were not addressed. The following year, the Daphnia species of zooplankton population increased due to the low population of their predominant predator—zooplankton-eating fish. The daphnia were then able to consume much of the algae and keep it under control, resulting in a clearer, cleaner lake. Some years later, due to rising external nutrient pollution, the natural systems were overloaded and the lake reverted back to a eutrophic state.

External pollution can be mitigated only up to a certain point, after which stopping/slowing pollution at the source remains the only option.

Observe your lake and surrounding shoreline for:

1) Water Clarity – If the water is not clear, you may want to test for nutrient levels.
2) Algae overgrowth
3) Type of vegetation, or lack thereof, around shoreline and littoral zone.

4) Buffer zones between the lake and roads, buildings, etc.

If there is a lack of proper vegetation in the littoral zone and shoreline, take the necessary steps to re-vegetate with the appropriate aquatic plants, as explained above.

If the water quality is extremely bad, check for external pollution sources: agricultural, industrial, and residential and commercial run-off, and proximity of septic systems to lake, as sewage may be seeping into the lake.

Try to pinpoint the source of pollution and take general steps to remedy. Talk to the offender(s) and present your case in a benefit-oriented way that he/she understands, and what they stand to gain by eliminating/reducing pollution entering the waterways. **Financial Benefits**: higher property values, better local economy, good public relations for the company, additional revenue from leasing the restored land etc. Also point out the health and recreation benefits. of a clean lake.

Help to set a precedent for other lake communities or districts to follow. Present your case to the appropriate governing bodies, emphasizing the health and financial returns.

Remediation Steps—Depending Upon Pollution Source

1) **Industrial** – If the industrial pollution source is identified, test the water at the source and in the lake. If you can prove the lake is contaminated from that specific site, you have a case to move forward. Contact the decision makers at the site and show the test results. Then explain how it is in their best interest to stop the flow of contaminants by itemizing tangible benefits to them (explained above). Outline proven ways to cut the pollution with constructed marshes, etc., and/or brainstorm other methods with the decision makers. If you are met with outright hostility, you may have to resort to creating a Bill of Rights for your local community and ecosystems to legally prevent industrial dumping. (See the follow-

ing chapter, Legal Rights of Ecosystems.)

2) **Agricultural** – Farms can follow the same procedures as industrial. You can reference whole farm practices using the New York watershed as an example, which is explained at the end of this chapter. These practices emphasized more efficient farming methods which saved both time and money, was healthier for the animals, and prevented agricultural runoff from entering the water supply.

If there are no obvious external pollution sources, look at the lake vegetation—or lack thereof. Is it barren, or are there a mixed variety of submerged, emergent, and shoreline plants? Are they native or invasive species? If there is a lack of vegetation, new plants can be introduced in several ways.

1) Arrange to have seedlings planted. Look at the beginning of this section for plant types and their benefits. Also, look at the constructed wetlands section and the water purifying qualities of the bulrush and other plants. Many municipalities offer these plants free of charge to lakefront property owners and even deliver to your doorstep. Check with your county for availability.
2) If your lake water levels have been kept relatively constant for many years, consider opening the dam to lower levels by several feet. As previously mentioned, the exposed mudflats will allow seeds to germinate. As the seedlings start to grow the water level can be raised again. Nature will grow the plants for you, if given the chance. Talk to the powers that be with regard to dam regulation and explain the cause-effect relationships.

Going to the Source

Most everyone would probably agree that it is more efficient and cost effective to solve problems as close to the source as possible. If that is the case, then why aren't stormwater and pollution runoff problems met head on where they originate, before they escalate into major complications? That is a rhetorical question, the real answer to which is most likely a political one and is beyond the scope of this book. The point here is that **you** can see the benefits of more efficient water management.

If each individual property (residential, commercial, big and small) was designed to absorb more of its own stormwater with rain gardens, constructed marshes, pervious pavement, etc., stormwater overflow and all the resulting problems would be history. Look at the hundreds of billions of dollars that would be saved—from expensive water infrastructure upgrades, to devalued properties, to major health costs.

Alternatives to conventional methods are all too quickly dismissed at planning board meetings. Equally overlooked are the many benefits of implementing such procedures. What are the health benefits to be able to swim without contracting an infection? How much additional tax revenue would result from clearer lakes? (See the section above on property value increases directly related to water clarity.) How about the resulting increase in tourism dollars or water sports-related business expansion?

The tired old lies still resound in those board meetings. If you want cleaner water, we have to raise taxes. Dirty water is a necessary by-product of "progress." Builders have been doing things a certain way for a long time and we can't change that. If you want to swim, put a pool in your back yard. These irrational comments are being told by people who are either afraid of speaking up and going against the status quo or are complicit in these destructive practices themselves. The people have been sold a bill of goods by developers, politicians, and industry.

Numbers don't lie. These upgrades need to be presented on pro forma income statements, specifying all cost reductions, expenses related to various types of upgrades, and projected revenues—5 to 10 years out. Then the present value of all net revenues can be calculated, eliminating most or all of the guesswork.

I recently attended a meeting of the North American Lake Management Society in Tampa, Florida. Most of the talk centered on "artificial" means of improving water quality, such as herbicide applications and mechanical aeration systems. One seminar in particular captured my full attention. This was a panel discussion about the protection of watersheds and the New York City drinking water supply. New York City has some of the best city water in the country, so they must be doing something better than most municipalities.

Federal law requires all drinking water to go through an expensive filtration process. New York watershed managers told the federal government they did not wish to go through that expense and that they had a cheaper, more efficient way to filter the water—one that prevented contamination from entering the water in the first place.

The problem was solved at the source, rather than treating toxic symptoms with ineffective water management. In this case, the primary source of pollution entering the watershed was agricultural run-off. Rather than let the contamination enter the watershed at all, it was decided to assist the local farmers in preventing agricultural runoff through what has been called "whole farm plans."

New York City Watershed Agricultural Program Whole Farm Planning is a partnership of city officials, farmers, and federal conservation agencies with the sole purpose of improving New York City's drinking water while implementing cleaner, more efficient, lower-cost farming methods.

Farmers who sign up agree to plan and develop a non-polluting, more holistic farming practice. The typical problems that are prioritized and managed are:

1) Parasites and phosphorus from animal waste
2) Phosphorus fertilizer storage
3) Pesticide mixing, loading areas, and applications
4) Excess nutrient runoff management

5) Manure management

In a case study written by the Department of Applied Economics and Management at Cornell University, the Whole Farms Bedded Pack Management System was proven effective in solving manure storage and runoff problems. Conventional farms typically store manure in large open areas, or "pools." This creates many problems such as the formation of methane gas and the manure seeping into groundwater aquifers, or directly into streams, rivers, and lakes. This system eliminated the need for such large pools and thus solved a major water contamination problem.

To summarize the procedure, more straw was added to the bedding areas of the cows, which was changed every other day with new straw. The old straw and manure was taken to a compost area where it was eventually applied to the fields as fertilizer. This was healthier for the cows as well, since they were mostly standing on soft straw rather than hard concrete floors. This may eliminate, or significantly reduce the hoof and leg problems associated with housing dairy cattle on concrete and other hard surfaces. Animal longevity and productivity would be expected to provide additional economic gains, but were not quantified due to the limitations of the study.

There are some additional up-front costs involved when implementing more sustainable agriculture, and since whole farm planning is a joint effort, municipalities and environmental agencies help defray the costs. In this case, New York City offered up to $75,000 for each farmer who implements a practical and sustainable plan. Given what the city would have paid to go through the federal water filtration process, money was saved. This is just one of many sustainable farming plans, which benefits all concerned—farmers, animals, municipalities, local residents, and ultimately everyone using the water.

Chapter Seven

Legal Rights of Ecosystems

The Earth Has a Right to an Attorney

> Communities and ecosystems possess the unalienable rights to exist, flourish, and evolve.
> – Ecuadorian Constitution

The Environmental Protection Agency, the environmental movement, green building, green this and that, energy conservation ... all are in a state of acute paralysis when it comes to affecting a real shift in favor of the natural world and healthy, fully-functioning, life-supporting ecosystems. The problem runs much deeper than imposing new laws restricting the amount of toxic substances allowed into the air/water/land each year. That is like saying we are not smart enough to avoid living in our own waste. We can't do it, or we won't do it? Let's face it, the problem can be solved, but not under the existing laws, which, for example, only "better regulate" polluters by allowing smaller amounts of poison into the water supply. Italian Architect Paolo Soleri referred to working **within** broken systems as a "*better kind of wrongness.*" Either through greed, hunger for power, ineptness, or plain stupidity, we continue with the "wrongness."

The rules of the game need to be changed across the board. The Community Environmental Legal Defense Fund (CELF) wrote in their recent newsletter:

> Our activism has failed to confront the basic premise of how our environmental laws actually function—that rather than protect the environment, they instead regulate its exploitation.

Prevailing thought is one of possessing, dominating, and imposing our will upon the natural world, with its complex (but extremely efficient and balanced) ecosystems and wildlife. There will be no change unless the natural world has rights to exist and flourish and is regarded on equal terms. Or, we raise our collective consciousness to one of inseparable unity with the natural world around us and treat all living beings and systems as natural extensions of ourselves.

The founding fathers consulted with and learned from the indigenous people of this country about pure democratic governance, some elements of which were included in the original Articles of Confederation of the United States, and to a lesser extent, the Constitution of the United States. We can (should) also learn how Native Americans related with the natural world and treated it as a complex, life-giving being with equal rights. How can we as a society move forward if our archaic laws do nothing more than try (mostly unsuccessfully) to limit amounts of toxic substances that can be released into the air, lakes, rivers, groundwater, etc.? In other words, its OK to live in a toxic cesspool as long as it doesn't kill everyone at once, just a few.

Nature is, for the most part, treated as a commodity. In the real estate appraisal profession, the "value" of land is based on its "highest and best use." Does highest and best mean what is best for the health of the people, ecosystem, or the wildlife living there? What is best for the neighboring homes and communities? What is best to maintain the purity of the aquifers? It is the highest and best use for the landowner and the landowner only, so long as no laws or ordinances are broken. It is the best use when it brings the highest monetary value to the owner only.

Should the natural world continue to be bought and sold in the open market with short or long-term monetary profit being the one and only criteria of value? I am most definitely in favor getting high monetary returns on your investment, but only when all costs have been factored into the equation. Since a strong economy is directly proportional to the health of its ecosystems, it stands to reason that any owner-inflicted degradation of those systems should become a liability to that owner, with the clean-up costs or any other remediation appearing as a debit on his balance sheet. It's a cost of doing business. If these costs were included in profit-loss statements and balance sheets, many of these transactions would not have taken place in the first place, as lower returns on investment would discourage investors. It would then behoove the sellers or buyers to create win-win solutions to these problems such as those outlined in this book.

Today's laws are no real deterrent to environmental degradation, as land owners, corporate or otherwise, are usually not directly culpable. These costs are rather spread out and paid indirectly through loss of open space, land/water pollution, traffic congestion, and higher taxes.

Carl Jung wrote that we all have dominant functions and that optimal physical and mental health requires development of those "neglected functions" for a well-rounded personality. That is to say, overdevelopment of rational, calculating, structured, linear language-based thinking dominates the neglected functions of intuition, feeling, and more "holistic" perspectives of deep connection with the surrounding environment. Plato referred to this as psyche kosmou. The Latin term anima mundi, or soul of the world, also describes this mode of thinking and awareness—the spiritual essence of the world as a living, sacred being.

This type of awareness is a "neglected function" in today's society. Indigenous cultures heard the trees, birds, clouds, sun, and mountains speaking to them as spirits. They listened to and felt the energy of nature. When these functions are developed, we become more sensitive to the natural living world. Natural systems become more valuable—far beyond immediate financial gain. The interrelatedness of human beings to the natural world then becomes more evident.

It boils down to one question. Is the earth and cosmos a living, sentient being that human beings are connected to on all levels? As such, is the earth worthy of our unconditional respect?

Modern "civilization" puts man at the center of the universe and yet apart from it—a dichotomy of being. Einstein wrote about "*the optical delusion of human consciousness with humanity at the center of existence.*" Our laws reflect this delusion. They are written based upon humans living above nature and dominating it.

Somehow, western man considers himself separate from the natural world. Quantum physics demonstrates there are no parts, but rather a complex, interconnected web in which the separate parts can only be understood within the context of the whole. Understanding and treating the land in this context supports our life-giving ecosystems while reducing costs. The bottom line is more profit with little or no damage to the surrounding land.

The question becomes, should we continue to treat the natural world as nothing more than a commodity? Not that long ago, it was perfectly acceptable to enslave free men and women, beat them into submission and subject them to a life of hard, forced labor. These slaves could be beaten and whipped at will, as they were the private "property" of the owners and had no rights.

We've evolved since then, but the life-supporting ecosystems of the world are in a similar quandary, because to this day, they have no rights. As long as man continues to feel entitled to exploit the natural world, ultimately to his own demise, there needs to be enforceable laws to protect those systems.

Before the colonization of Africa and the introduction of English custom law, there were no "objects," and everything was considered alive—the sky, the mountains, the water, plants and animals, and the balance between them needed to be maintained for all life to flourish, man included. All species had rights, responsibilities, and duties, where none were considered above any other, and all needed each other for the system to live. This unwritten, traditional law was passed down from generation to generation. It was a way of life and usually never questioned. This is similar to the natural law of Native Americans. (See Sacred Lands chapter).

A recent Kenyan Draft Constitution was drawn up in order to bring these eco/earth-centric laws back into the current mainstream legal system. It ultimately drew a lot of support, but was narrowly defeated in the end. Regardless of the Draft Constitution's outcome, the people of Kenya realized that their traditional customary law was required on some level to help solve modern-day problems.

It would seem counter intuitive to have politicians and special interest groups draft legislation to protect the natural world. They may mean well, but their expertise and motivations typically regard these biological systems as secondary to the accumulation of power and material wealth. They most probably do not understand the complex interrelationships of plant and animal life, or the cause and effect of certain actions given those relationships. Many indigenous cultures view all these things as alive, and spiritual. Therefore, input from these people should be considered in these lawmaking decisions. The South African Environmental Management Act did just that. Indigenous people, including women and children, were made an integral part of the lawmaking process. It included laws that considered nature on equal terms with man.

Consider a clear, pristine, healthy lake/ecosystem, which recently degraded into a weed/disease-infested, mosquito-breeding, toxic body of water, dotted with bloated, floating fish—easy to find these days. Typically, this is the result of sewage overflow, pesticide/fertilizer runoff, and oil, grease, and chemical seepage into the lake from nearby residential and/or commercial mixed-use development. Sadly, this is more the norm than the exception to the rule. Researchers from the U.S. Geological Survey (USGS) and the U.S. Environmental Protection Agency (EPA) found that one-third of U.S. water systems contain traces of at least 18 unregulated and potentially hazardous contaminants, many of which are linked to endocrine disruption and cancer.

Look at the larger context from a new perspective, devoid of jaded excuses and limited beliefs. What if the natural world had a voice, legal representation, and laws that would stand up in the current legal system? What if the aforementioned lake and all life in it were protected by laws against its degradation and/or destruction. What would that mean for your children to swim in a crystal clear lake? What would it mean to their health and welfare? How would that affect the quality of drinking water in the area? What would be the economic benefits in terms of property values and business expansion? What health care costs could be avoided without contaminated water exposure? How would the overall quality of life improve? How would wildlife be affected? These questions are rarely asked. People have become numbed to the idea of dirty water, air, and soil being necessary and inevitable side effects of economic development and "progress."

A complete paradigm shift that redefines man's relationship to the natural world may be in order—where ecosystems and all other life have equal rights to exist and flourish—where nature is no longer considered a commodity to be exploited. The tiny country of Ecuador included such language in their Constitution, which is partially stated as follows:

Rights of Nature Articles in Ecuador's Constitution

Title II Fundamental Rights Chapter 1

Entitlement, Application and Interpretation Principles of the Fundamental Rights

Art.10. Rights Entitlement

Persons and people have the fundamental rights guaranteed in this Constitution and in the international human rights instruments. Nature is subject to those rights given by this Constitution and Law.

Chapter 7: Rights for Nature
Art. 71. Nature or Pachamama
Where life is reproduced and exists, has the right to exist, persist, maintain and regenerate its vital cycles, structure, functions and its processes in evolution.
Every person, people, community or nationality, will be able to demand the recognitions of rights for nature before the public organisms. The application and interpretation of these rights will follow the related principles established in the Constitution.
The State will motivate natural and juridical persons as well as collectives to protect nature; it will promote respect towards all the elements that form an ecosystem.
Art. 72. Nature Has the Right to Restoration
This integral restoration is independent of the obligation on natural and juridical persons or the State to indemnify the people and the collectives that depend on the natural systems.

Local governments and communities around the U.S. and world are doing just that. Independent-thinking communities and townships are now defying the status quo and rewriting their local ordinances to give legal rights to the land, water, air, and ecosystems.

There are many hurdles to overcome, especially in a legal system where commerce trumps environmental protections. The U.S. government and economic system was originally based in English common law, which was written to facilitate the expansion of the British empire. This included more centralized power and commodification of natural resources for economic and military gain

The original United States Articles of Confederation were written with a more "democratic" system in mind. The document was more in line with the Iroquois Confederation system of government than English common law (see chapter 2). However, the articles underwent major revisions to better represent the philosophies of the "founding fathers," many of whom were wealthy landowners or industrialists. A document more in line with English law best served their purposes. The result was the U.S. Constitution.

The following chart shows some differences between the Articles of Confederation and the U.S. Constitution.

Articles of Confederation

- States are sovereign—no centralized, pre-emptive government over states
- Congress had no power over interstate or foreign commerce
- No independent executive—it took nine states to agree to go to war
- No Federal Courts—only state governments acted directly on the people
- No taxing power given to Congress

U.S. Constitution

- Central Federal government can act directly on the people
- The Commerce Clause regulates interstate and foreign commerce over states
- Independent Executive chose by electoral college
- The Federal Supreme Court is the highest court with most authority
- Congress has power to lay and collect taxes, duties, and excises

The Constitution had provisions for more centralized power and control—many controlled by the relative few. It worked for the British Empire, and many of our founding fathers had a vested interest in that system. Alexander Hamilton thought British government was the best model for the colonies. James Madison argued that states be under control of the Federal government, and that the best form of government was a limited monarchy. He went on to say "an extensive republic" over the 13 states would more easily control the factional struggles resulting from inequalities of wealth.

Why are these current laws worth mentioning? Because they make it difficult for local governments and communities to control their own destinies and to protect their land, water, and ecosystems from fracking, strip mining, factory farming, clear cutting, toxic waste dumping, etc.

Attempts have been made by local communities to prevent such practices. They tried to work within the existing regulatory system, only to discover they were virtually powerless to prevent corporate polluters. They were powerless because our legal framework emphasizes economic development over local concerns. According to the late historian Howard Zinn: "

> When economic interest is seen behind political clauses of the Constitution, then the document becomes not only the work of wise men trying to establish a decent and orderly society, but the work of certain groups trying to maintain their privileges, while giving just enough rights and privileges to enough of the people to insure popular support.

The Constitution has specific provisions, which diminish the rights of local governments and citizens.

1) **Commerce Clause** – This was enacted to promote more interstate and foreign commerce, and only congress has the authority to regulate interstate commerce. For example, if a township or state wants to stop the trucking in and dumping of sludge from another state, they would be, in effect, preventing interstate commerce. The commercial value of dumping sludge into an ecosystem is, under the constitution, held

in higher regard than the health of the ecosystem. All nature is considered "property" and a commodity under the law, including sludge. Today, environmental protections come under the authority of the Commerce Clause. That is to say, if certain bodies of water, ecosystems, etc., are needed for interstate commerce, their protections are either severely limited or nonexistent.

2) **Dillon's Rule** – allows a state legislature to control local government structure, methods of financing its activities and its procedures, and the authority to undertake functions. This amendment creates a hierarchy of power, starting at the state level and ending with local governments and communities having the least power.
3) **The 14th Amendment** – gives corporations personhood and with it the rights of people. Corporate lawyers can argue that their clients' rights to free trade are being discriminated against if, as in the example above, sludge dumping is not allowed but other types of businesses are. Also, section 1983 of the Constitution allows persons (corporations) to sue for damages if their rights were violated.

If a regulatory system does not serve your interests, it is nearly impossible to work within it. The solution then is to create a new one. Thomas Jefferson said the Constitution should be changed with every generation, that protest and challenges to the law are healthy. In this spirit, many communities are refusing to play within a legal system that does not adequately represent them. Rather, they are creating a new set of laws that better serve their communities—laws that challenge doctrines such as the 14th Amendment and Commerce Clause. They are writing their own Bills of Rights, with rights for ecosystems to exist and flourish, rights to clean air and water, etc. They are creating an entirely new paradigm for all life within their communities—no more tiptoeing around archaic laws. They are challenging their outright existence.

The Community Environmental Legal Defense Fund, a non-profit legal firm, wrote the Rights of Nature Ordinance which "rcognizes that natural communities and ecosystems possess an inalienable and fundamental right to exist and flourish and that residents of those communities possess the legal authority to enforce those rights on behalf of those ecosystems…" In addition, these laws "require the governmental apparatus to remedy violations of those ecosystem rights." Their work includes helping townships around the country write new local ordinances. The validity of these new ordinances are now being debated in several state supreme courts. If recognized, these laws will legally prevent the destruction of the environment and ecosystems in a particular district as well as put the power of the region back into the hands of local people, rather than corporations.

Lake Erie Bill of Rights

The Lake Erie ecosystem has suffered major damage over the years, usually from agricultural runoff and industrial waste entering the lake in a raw, untreated state. A citizen put together the Lake Erie Bill of Rights which gives citizens the right to sue any polluters whose actions harm the health of the ecosystem, and its right to exist and flourish. On December 4, 2018 the Toledo, Ohio City Council voted unanimously to place the proposed Lake Erie Bill of Rights law onto the ballot for a vote.

In February, 2019 the citizens voted the Bill of Rights into law. This gave the lake and all its ecosystems rights to a healthy existence, and that anyone violating those rights by polluting or in some destroying the ecological balance would be subject to penalty under the law. According to the Community Environmental Legal Defense Fund Attorneys:

> This Lake Erie Bill of Rights is the first proposed law to advance

> in the U.S. that specifically focuses on a distinct ecosystem, securing the Lake's rights to exist and flourish.

On February 29, 2020 the US District Court for the Northern District of Ohio ruled that the **Lake Erie Bill of Rights was "invalid in its entirety."**

District Judge Jack Zouhary found that, while the goal was well-intended, the law itself was "*unconstitutionally vague and exceeded the power of municipal government in Ohio.*" He sympathized with the residents of Toledo and went on to say that "*with careful drafting, Toledo probably could enact valid legislation to reduce water pollution,*"

This exemplifies constitutional laws and amendments that value commerce over human life, and render municipal governments and the will of their people powerless in the face of corporate interests. Since the passage of the Bill of Rights in February, it has come under attack by:

- **The Ohio House of Representatives**
  This body adopted its 2020-2021 budget with provisions that prohibit anyone, including local governments, from enforcing recognized legal rights for ecosystems.
- **Ohio Governor Mike Dewine**
  signed a 2500+ page state budget bill which includes language that attempts to abolish Rights of Nature law in Ohio, including: "No person, on behalf of or representing nature or an ecosystem, shall bring an action in any court of common pleas"
- **Franklin County Ohio Board of Elections**
  refused to place duly qualified Community Bill of Rights citizen initiative on the November ballot
- **Ohio Chamber of Commerce**
  Zachary Frymier, Director of Energy and Environmental Policy for the Ohio Chamber of Commerce wrote law banning rights of nature enforcement.

Legal Battles over Fracking

Fracking is a process that injects millions of gallons of highly pressurized water, chemicals and sand into the ground in order to create cracks or fissures in the bedrock to let the natural gas escape. Chemicals found in these fluids include diesel fuel, acetone, and acids, many of which cause major health problems, including cancer. The water is pumped underground not only from the initial injection, but also from the resulting waste water that is easily disposed of by forcing it back into the ground.

A Community Bill of Rights Ordinance for Grant Township, PA, was adopted on June 3, 2014, in response to the Pennsylvania General Energy Company's (PG&E) plans to extract oil via fracking in the region. This bill prohibits the injecting of oil and gas waste material into the underground water supply as a result of fracking. This is in direct conflict with the U.S. Constitution, which gives corporations the rights of people. As a person, a corporation is granted "equal protection" under the 14th Amendment. Therefore, any corporation such as PG&E that is singled out and discriminately prevented from doing business is a violation of the 14th Amendment.

PG&E exercised those federal constitutional rights and sued Grant Township to overturn their local Bill of Rights. PG&E claimed that the local Bill of Rights violates their constitutional right to conduct business within the township. The lawsuit contained 11 counts against Grant Township, including, but not limited to:

Supremacy Clause Violation

The Supremacy Clause of the Sixth Amendment of the United States Constitution establishes that the United States Constitution and federal law are "the supreme Law of the Land" having precedent over state laws, and even state constitutions.

Equal Protection Clause Violation

The Equal Protection Clause of the Fourteenth Amendment of

the United States Constitution provides that no state shall "deny to any person within its jurisdiction the equal protection of the laws." The purpose of the Equal Protection Clause is to protect every person within a state's jurisdiction against arbitrary discrimination occasioned by the express terms of a statute or by its improper execution through duly constituted agents.

First Amendment Violation

The First Amendment of the United States Constitution provides that no law shall abridge "the right of the people . . . to petition the Government for a redress of grievances." The Community Bill of Rights Ordinance purports to divest corporations, such as PG&E, of their constitutional right to petition the government for a redress of grievances in that it strips corporations of: (1) their status as "persons" under the law; (2) their right to assert state or federal preemptive laws in an attempt to overturn the Community Bill of Rights Ordinance; and (3) their power to assert that Grant Township lacks the authority to adopt the Community Bill of Rights Ordinance.

According to the Community Environmental Legal Defense Fund: "The ordinance secures community rights to local self-governance, and clean air and water, by banning injection wells." Resident Judy Wanchisn reaffirmed that "pure water is guaranteed to us by the Pennsylvania Constitution under article 1, section 27."

In 2017, the Department of Environmental Protection **issued a permit to legalize a frack waste water injection well in Grant Township, Pennsylvania. and simultaneously sued the township.** The agency claimed that Grant's Home Rule Charter – which protects the local environment – interfered with the DEP's authority to administer state oil and gas policy.

A Surprising Reversal in Policy

In March 2020 the DEP reversed their decision to allow fracking. They went on to say, "Grant Township's Home Rule Charter bans the injection of oil and gas waste fluids," "Therefore, the operation of the Yanity well as an oil and gas waste fluid injection well would violate that applicable law."

This could very well set off a chain of precedents in communities' ability to prohibit the contamination of their water supplies for corporate profit.

Colorado Mining

On May 22, 2014, the Colorado ballot initiative 75—Right to Local Self Government—was presented to the Colorado Supreme Court. The Colorado Community Rights Network (COCRN) then collected enough signatures for initiative 75 to qualify for the November 2014 ballot. This initiative states, "People have an inherent and inalienable right to local self-government," and that the current legal framework, which enables corporations to preempt local ordinances, threatens the essence of democracy. The amendment did **not** make the November 4, 2014, ballot in Colorado as an initiated constitutional amendment.

The Colorado Mining Association used their preemptive rights to reverse a five-county ban on the use of cyanide in gold mining. The same tactics are being used against the towns of Longmont, Lafayette, and Ft. Collins, Colorado, to overturn efforts to prohibit fracking and other polluting gas and oil extraction methods.

One needs to step back and look at this again. Current laws prohibit citizens from preventing the injection of cyanide into their water supply. Suicidal people take cyanide capsules to kill themselves. It makes one wonder what kinds of individuals would sign these preemptive laws into power. What is their agenda?

Maplight, an independent nonprofit organization that reports federal lobbying disclosure filings, showed that the U.S. Chamber of Commerce was number one in total lobbying money spent in the first quarter of 2015 at $13,800,000. This may have a bearing on some lawmakers' reluctance to prevent corporations from conducting interstate commerce on any level, no matter what the consequences to the local environment, economies, or citizen health.

In sparsely populated Mora County, New Mexico, county commissioners passed the community water rights and local self-governance ordinances. This banned oil and gas drilling/extraction anywhere in Mora County. Shortly thereafter, the Independent Petroleum Association of New Mexico and three local property owners filed lawsuits against the county. It was soon followed with another lawsuit filed by Shell Western, a division of Royal Dutch Shell. They argued Shell's rights were being violated because the ordinance criminalized Shell's primary business function—the extraction of gas and oil.

The case went to court where U.S. District Judge James Browning wrote that Mora County had a "legitimate county interest" in protecting the county from damage as a result of oil and gas extraction. However, the court found that the New Mexico Oil and Gas Act preempts the ordinance, and that even a temporary moratorium on oil and gas drilling would violate that Act.

Judge Browning said that corporations have these rights and that the District Court did not have the authority to change them. He went on to write: "The Defendants arguments that corporations should not be granted constitutional rights, or that corporate rights should be subservient to peoples' rights, are arguments that are best made before the Supreme Court—the only court that can overrule Supreme Court precedent, rather than District Court."

Fracking Outlawed in Mansfield, Ohio

There was a different outcome in Ohio, where local citizens exercised their right to self-government and a clean, healthy environment. In November 2012, by a vote of 62.87% in favor, the people of the City of Mansfield, in north-central Ohio and home to nearly 48,000 people, adopted an amendment to their home rule charter that recognizes a community Bill of Rights and allows for the prohibition of the injection of frack wastewater. This was in response to the Ohio Department of Natural Resources granting permits for Preferred Fluids Management, LLC to dig 5,000-foot injection wells in Mansfield's industrial park.

City council member Scott Hazen said, "The citizens of Mansfield were not, in any way, shape or form, asked whether or not this was something that was appropriate and we were not in any way consulted as to whether or not this could, potentially, cause long-term damage to our city. So I take great offense to the fact that the State made the blanket appropriation of our land without giving us any sort of recourse."

Cindy Soliday of Frack Free Ohio and Frack Free Mansfield contacted the Community Environmental Legal Defense Fund to help draft the charter amendment for Mansfield. There was little opposition to the amendment and it eventually passed.

There were some repercussions from the American Petroleum Institute, the Ohio Chamber of Congress, and the group Energy Citizens after the amendment passed, but that was short lived. The people of Mansfield exercised their rights to local self-governance and their inalienable rights to clean air, water, and a healthy environment.

When asked about the victory for Mansfield, Cindy Soliday replied, "The voice of the people is always paramount. I am very proud of my community and that democracy lives and breathes in Mansfield Ohio. Our hope is that the precedent set with the passage of our Bill of Rights, will empower other communities to enact similar legislation to assert the right to self-govern."

New Hampshire town defends itself against big oil

On March 12, 2013, the town of Grafton, New Hampshire, implemented a newly drafted ordinance that granted the local citizens a "fundamental and inalienable right to protect and preserve the scenic, historic, and aesthetic values of the town." It also granted the people a "right to self-governance." This ordinance also gave natural communities and ecosystems within the town the inalienable right to exist and flourish. If there were any violations against these ecosystems, the citizens of the town would have the legal standing to enforce those laws.

This all started when a large Spanish energy company was planning to operate in and around Grafton. Enraged citizens immediately went out and got enough signatures to put a new Community Bill of Rights on the agenda for that year's meeting. It passed, and the town successfully defended itself against energy companies operating in their area.

Punch-Counter Punch

On January 9, 2013, the Board of Supervisors of Highland Township in Elk County, Pennsylvania, unanimously adopted an ordinance that established a community Bill of Rights and forbids corporations "to deposit, store, treat, inject, or process waste water, 'frack' water, brine or other materials, chemicals or by-products that have been used in the extraction of shale gas onto or into the land, air, or waters within Highland Township." This prohibition specifically applies to disposal injection wells.

Will the letter of the law trump the spirit of true freedom and independence? Not if the energy companies have anything to do with it. Seneca Resources Corp., an oil and gas extraction company, and later the Department of Environmental Protection sued Highland Township saying their Bill or Rights Home Charter violated state law. Right now, it's punch-counter punch—the constitutional rights of corporations vs. the rights of residents to local self-governance, a clean environment, and the pursuit of happiness.

Susan Paradise Baxter, United States Magistrate Judge, made the following ruling in September 2017.:

> Nothing in either of these sworn Declarations provides evi

> dence that these proposed Intervenors have suffered or will suffer a concrete and particularized injury-in-fact so as to have standing here. The alleged injury is speculative, at best, and because it involves a heightened risk of future harm, the allegations are required to "entail a degree of risk sufficient to meet the concreteness requirement." Kamal, 2016 WL 6133827.
> CACHE (Citizens Advocating a Clean Healthy Environment) and the Ecosystem's interests in this case are based solely on their desire to defend the Home Rule Charter. No evidence has been produced to demonstrate that any claimed future injury is directly traceable to repealing or affirming the Home Rule Charter. Accordingly, CACHE and the Ecosystem have failed to meet their burden to demonstrate standing for purposes of intervention as of right. Finally, and alternatively, these proposed Intervenors have requested that this Court grant them permissive intervention. Because CACHE and the Ecosystem have not established standing, this Court will deny their request for permissive intervention.

The Township eventually repealed their ordinance and entered into a settlement with Seneca Resources Corp. The battles continue over local citizens demand for clean air and water vs. the state, Federal Government and corporations exercising their rights under the 14th amendment, Commerce Clause and Dillons Rule. It's a gray area now and will probably remain so until new language is added to state and Federal legislation that gives local municipalities more control over their health and welfare and the environment in which they reside.

This language already appears in the Philippine Constitution, which made it easier for a group of citizens in the Philippines to win a class-action lawsuit against timber companies for destroying the natural ecosystems and jeopardizing the health of the citizens. The judge ruled in favor of the plaintiffs, based upon the rights of the citizens to a "balanced and healthful ecology" as written in their Constitution:

Section 16, Article II of their 1987 Constitution explicitly provides: "The State shall protect and advance the right of the people to a balanced and healthful ecology in accord with the rhythm and harmony of nature." This right unites with the right to health which is provided for in the preceding section of the same article: "The State shall protect and promote the right to health of the people and instill health consciousness among them."

India's Constitution has also evolved to prevent environmental devastation. The new language under Article 21 of their Constitution is more about an expanded view of life than preventing specific offenses, an umbrella if you will, under which all life and natural systems are respected. It reads as follows:

> Article 21 protects right to life as a fundamental right. Enjoyment of life and its attainment, including their right to life with human dignity encompasses within its ambit, the protection and preservation of environment, ecological balance free from pollution of air and water... Any contra acts or actions that would cause environmental, ecological, air, water, pollution, etc., should be regarded as amounting to violation of Article 21.12.

The ecosystems of the world need better legal representation, and these are all steps in that direction. Thomas Jefferson said civil disobedience is not only healthy but necessary and that the Constitution should be changed with every generation. Archaic laws misrepresenting the spirit of the law are meant to be rewritten. They should embrace all life, and not perpetuate destruction, disease, and death.

To Sum Up...

Today's U.S. Federal laws, including the Commerce Clause, right to preemption, corporations given rights as persons, among others, tip the scales in favor of corporate exploitation and the many negative side effects. Some countries, as mentioned earlier, have already put language in their constitutions that provides equal rights to the environment and protects the health and welfare of local citizens

This begs the question, why is the U.S. dragging its feet on these issues? You can be diligent and research the money trail, political lobbying, misinformation passed on as truth by mainstream media, and any other reasons. Real solutions that actually benefit all life on this planet are never discussed in the corporate-controlled mainstream media — technologies that are low cost, non-polluting, and efficient.

For example, the Brillion Energy Corporation developed a system using solid state low energy nuclear reaction (LENR) which releases no emissions, and no radioactive waste. This is fusion, not the nuclear fission reactors being used today, which also require the mining of uranium for its fuel rods, and using massive amounts of water to keep the system from overheating. or melting down. In LENR cold fusion technology, hydrogen atoms are fused into helium which releases excess heat energy. Hydrogen is abundant everywhere. According to Brillion, there is enough hydrogen in a single glass of water to power hundreds of homes, even thousands, if the hydrogen to heat conversion is efficient enough.

What about the work of Nikola Tesla? Where are all his patents on energy, including the use of magnets and the earth's natural electrical charge to create a clean, abundant energy supply? Whether they were perfected or not, those technologies would be worth examining. More on this later.

Mahatma Gandhi defeated the British Empire through respectful dialogue and nonviolent actions. If enough people apply sustainable principles to their real estate while reaping the benefits from doing so, a groundswell of change at the local level may/should eventually make its way to the highest levels of government.

The balance of power in the United States starts at the top with the federal government, then state, and local. It should come as no surprise that local communities, being low on the totem pole, are having such a hard time stopping corporate polluters. Corporations engaged in interstate commerce (in-state commerce is controlled by the states under the 10th Amendment to the Constitution) are protected by federal law, which reigns supreme in the U.S. on these types of issues. Abraham Lincoln warned about imbalance of power:

> I see in the near future a crisis approaching that unnerves me and causes me to tremble for the safety of our country. Corporations have been enthroned and an era of corruption in high places will follow, and the money power of the country will endeavor to prolong its reign by working upon the prejudices of the people until all wealth is aggregated in a few hands and the Republic is destroyed.

That said, there are scattered victories for the local communities and their Bills of Rights, as referenced earlier. As more and more local communities vote in their own Bills of Rights, it may only be a matter of time before they become part of their respective state constitutions. Eventually, similar language may appear at the federal level, and thus ending the costly, time-consuming legal battles that now rage on.

Laws are meant to evolve with the times. We didn't have the water crises (California had a mandatory 25% reduction in water usage in some areas) and other environmental disasters of today when the Constitution was written or when the preemption clause or commerce clauses were added. The framers (some of them, anyway) of the Constitution were concerned about representing all the people, so why shouldn't locally written bills of rights and ordinances be considered more in the national and state debates? Thomas Jefferson, a proponent of equal representation said: "*The hand of the people ... has power that government to be the strongest of which every man feels himself a part.*"

The Burden of Proof

In July, 2017 a group of citizens in Spokane, Washington tried to prevent the rail transport of fossil fuel through the city, a major hub for distribution to the Northwest. The lawsuit, Holmquist et al v. United States, asserted that federal preemption over local municipal control over oil and coal shipments violated their constitutional rights to a healthy climate and local self-government. This directly challenged federal preemption law and the Supremacy clause of the Constitution (Article VI of the U.S. Constitution) which states, "the Constitution and the laws of the United States ... shall be the supreme law of the land ... anything in the Constitutions or laws of any State to the contrary notwithstanding."

The U.S. District Court Eastern District of Washington dismissed the action due, but not limited to, lack of standing, and because the issue was not ripe. A party has standing only if they incurred "injury in fact," and that the injury is fairly traceable to the action being challenged. The injury or threat of injury must be "real and immediate, not conjectural or hypothetical." A claim is not "ripe" if it rests upon contingent future events that may or may not occur.

Local governments would be well advised to compile any and all evidence to strengthen their legal standing. Medical records, air/water samples, expert testimony, etc. Since the dismissal of this case was based primarily on lack of standing, the right documentation may have changed the ruling. This in turn could set a precedent for future rulings.

A similar case was ruled in favor of the plaintiffs. A recent federal court decision in Oregon recognized that citizens have a "right to a livable climate" in accordance with the due process clause of the U.S. Constitution. Here judge Ann Aiken of the U.S. District Court for the

District of Oregon wrote, "*I have no doubt that the right to a climate system capable of sustaining human life is fundamental to a free and ordered society ... to hold otherwise would be to say the Constitution affords no protection against a government's knowing decision to poison the air its citizens breath or the water its citizens drink.*"

Getting Out of Our Own Way

Trying to change a legal system that has been in place for hundreds of years and that is designed to perpetuate its original intentions is a slow process. Current laws, for the most part, give no voice to the natural world and place man on a pedestal—blind and deaf to the natural forces around him. It is time to wake up.

Yes, inroads have been made worldwide to rewrite these archaic laws as explained above, but change in the highest courts has yet to happen, with the exception of Ecuador. New perception and awareness would most probably facilitate this process—a perception of the world through the eyes of other living beings where man can see and understand the living universe from perspectives other than his or her own, and undistorted by an egotistic sense of entitlement.

Indigenous cultures listen to the rivers, mountains, trees, and animals. There is communication through energy and sounds, as everything is alive. So-called civilized man knows and benefits from this as well. Theodore Roosevelt said, "Wilderness itself is the basis of all our civilization. I wonder if we have enough reverence for life to concede to wilderness the right to live on." Henry David Thorough wrote of similar experiences in his classic Walden Pond. The list is endless, yet our laws are written and enforced as if none of this matters.

Narrow, specialized, funnel vision-type thinking (as opposed to feeling, intuitive, right-brain, everything interconnected approach) dominates our culture, to the point where all else is secondary. Albert Einstein said:

> We should take care not to make the intellect our God. It has, of course, powerful muscles, but no personality. It cannot lead, it can only serve.

There is a story that took place in Kenya that gives nature a voice, and views the world from a different perspective. It is seen through the eyes of a hyena.

It begins with a starving female hyena looking for food to feed herself and newborn. Food was scarce due to over-building and drought. She came upon a farmer's goat pen and started looking around for food. The farmer immediately came out with a shotgun and killed the hyena. A court case ensued where both the farmer and hyena were equally represented. The court argued that the hyena was only trying to survive and feed her young. The farmer did not have to kill the hyena and could have just as easily chased her away. The court ruled that the farmer's actions were cruel and extreme. An appropriate punishment was enforced.

The bottom line is that as long as modern man considers himself superior and above all other life, including indigenous people, the existing laws will take time to change, as there are long-standing precedents to overcome and strong resistance by the people in power who like things just as they are.

It should be obvious that change in favor of life and health over commerce and profit will happen from the bottom up, as evidenced by the hard fought victories by local community rights organizations. However, commerce/profit **can** coexist with life and health. Rather than making minor, insignificant changes to a flawed system, by limiting amounts of contamination, sewer overflow, erosion, etc. the entire system should be designed to prevent, or significantly reduce the chances of these problems from happening at all. Yes, our laws allow corporate exploitation and pollution to continue, and yes, we need the energy. However, where is the discussion about other highly efficient energy sources? And I am **not** talking about solar panels or wind farms.

Years ago, Croatian electrical engineer and physicist Nikola Tesla obtained over 200 patents on free, alternative electrical generation. Many such inventions condensed and turned into electricity the tremendous electrical force that exists between the positively charged sun (with a potential of 200 billion volts) and the negatively charged earth. This force is what he called cosmic energy. In 1931 Tesla was quoted in the press, saying "I have harnessed the cosmic rays and caused them to operate a motive device. More than 25-years-ago I began my efforts to harness the cosmic rays and I have succeeded. Electric power is everywhere present, in unlimited qualities. This new power for the driving of the world's machinery will be derived from the energy which operates in the universe, without the need for coal, gas, oil, or any other fuel."

What happened to all of these patents and why aren't they (and others) in the energy conversation today? Rather, we focus on expensive, dirty options like gas, coal, oil, solar panels and batteries (look at the rare earth mineral extraction required for these.) and inefficient and disruptive wind farms.

If the peoples' best interests were being addressed, these patents would be made available to our free enterprise system where one individual or company would most certainly improve upon it and/or make it commercially available. That does not happen today, because the current power structure wants to maintain its control—at the expense of all life on the planet.

Thomas Jefferson's maintained that the strongest government is one in which "every man feels a part," and that laws need to change and evolve with the times. Broaden the discussion to include more self-governance, while expanding upon (without bias) technological innovation for energy, and political participation will most probably skyrocket.

Chapter Eight

Land Planning and Development

Merging with Surrounding Ecosystems

In an arcology, the built environment and the living processes of the inhabitants interact as organs, tissues, and cells do in a highly evolved organism.
- Paolo Soleri

One cannot argue with the fact that most all municipalities in this country lack necessary funds for proper infrastructure maintenance. Antiquated sewer systems regularly overflow, roads and bridges are in need repair, power lines require maintenance, etc. When the need arises to update any of these systems, the typical response is that there is no money to do it.

Why is this? The answer lies in development priorities, subsidies, and property tax structure. The current system encourages new, glitzy developments, both residential and commercial, over sustainable retrofits and additions to existing structures and/or strategic land use in downtown and nearby areas. Larger developments and new buildings normally take priority in most cities and townships for several erroneous reasons:

- Big and new is perceived as better
- Larger developments have more financial backing and can more easily cut through legal red tape
- There is the illusion that large, new developments will

bring in more tax revenue compared with smaller, existing building renovations

- These types of developments are equated with economic prosperity

Now we will look at the numbers and see how new development, big box stores in particular, generate far less revenue for the municipality than investment in downtown retrofits. Charles Marohn, an engineer and land use planner in Minnesota, analyzed why cities and municipalities across the country are, for the most part, broke. In his excellent book, "Strong Towns," he researched various types of properties and the tax revenue they create. His analysis was based on tax dollars generated **per acre**, rather than the total taxes paid. This seems to be a better way to demonstrate a property's efficiency and productivity from a tax revenue standpoint.

Sprawling big box stores outside city limits take up a lot of land, and when you calculate total taxes paid per acre, it is substantially less than smaller, older buildings in downtown areas. Given this reality, government officials remain reluctant to invest in retrofits when a big box store wants to build a new facility in their backyard. And, with this new facility comes new infrastructure expenses in the form of roads, sewer and water lines, electric, phone lines..., Most of this is on the developer, but down the road it is the city or county's responsibility to keep it maintained, and at great expense.

Marohn illustrates this with three commercial properties in High Point, North Carolina. A new, massive Wal Mart was built on the outskirts of High Point. The tax revenue it generated was $968,000 per acre per year. A nearby K-Mart generated $385,000 per acre. A small pizzeria in downtown High Point generated much less total revenue, but its tax revenue **per acre came to $3,450,000.** This scenario is typical throughout the United States.

What is the better investment for the city, to invest in downtown, or throw-away buildings on the outskirts? Let's face it, when the building starts to deteriorate, Wal Mart will pack up, leave and repeat the process all over again somewhere else. Why? because most towns are happy to have a brand-new Wal Mart, and will pay them to come to their areas in the form of tax subsidies. Also, constructing a big box store is relatively inexpensive compared to other building types, thus making them expendable.

I will play devil's advocate now. One may think that as long as the Wal mart is generating more **total** tax dollars, it would be better for the city. This is not the case, if you look at the overall value of the land itself. Let us assume the land was a completely undeveloped, wooded area. What is the true value of that land in its virgin state? What overall impact does that land have on the surrounding areas and entire region with regard to finance and health? These questions are rarely ever asked in planning board meetings where NEW development is the mantra and undeveloped land is there to be "improved."

Here are just a few things to take into consideration before calling in the bulldozers:

1) Unspoiled open land adds value to the entire area, as open space and parkland is both desirable and necessary for a higher quality of life.
2) Properties backing up to this "preserve" are valued much higher than similar-type properties in a typical subdivision.
3) Flood mitigation. Wooded areas have excellent absorptive qualities for stormwater drainage, thus reducing the need for additional stormwater piping infrastructure.
4) Air and Water purification
5) Soil erosion prevention

What is the financial impact of all these? What is the total cost of flooding to buildings in terms of clean-up, insurance premiums, the stigma that comes with a flood prone area, etc. These are costs/

savings not factored into revenue projections for new developments. There are other benefits covered in detail throughout this book.

We tend to take land for granted, until there is no more. Most developers indiscriminately bulldoze vast tracks of virgin forest into desolate badlands and then build inefficient, identical "boxes" with no regard for location, climate, topography, vegetation, etc. Our senses are gradually being dulled to accept more and more noise, pollution, and congestion. That is more a function of poor planning and management than over-population.

If such tracts of land generate revenue in and of itself with no construction, then wouldn't it make sense to leave it alone and retrofit an existing building for a Wal Mart (if you really have to have it) in or closer to a downtown area? Yes, it makes perfect financial and logistical sense as it presents the best of both worlds:

- more overall tax revenue for the city
- more open, unspoiled land
- higher tax value for existing properties on the outskirts of town

The logistical problems of a big box store in the downtown area could be solved with the following scenario. Assuming there was enough commercial space available downtown, the Wal Mart could move in there. If they needed additional space they could always expand back, or up. Let's assume they needed an extra 5,000 square feet; they could knock out the back walls and build new space there, or add another level. This would preserve the look and feel of the downtown area since the storefront would still blend right in with the rest of the street. With regard to parking, or lack thereof, a multi-level parking facility could be constructed, maybe in place of old abandoned buildings close by, or on otherwise unused land. This could also bring in additional revenue as a city parking garage.

Creating a "living roof" (see the Sustainable Building section) would add more usable space on the rooftop in a relaxing environment of plants and grasses for eating, drinking, exercise, or just taking in the city landscape from above. Aside from the aesthetics and additional space for customers and workers, living roofs add many years to the rooftop's life while providing better insulation from heat and cold. Utility bills go down, as do roof repair/replacement costs. There are many other steps that can be taken to bring more profitability, resilience, and efficiency to buildings, as outlined throughout this book,

A good PR campaign could promote all this and help change the stigma of Wal Mart as downtown-wrecking, land-spoiling corporate giant with no regard for the local economy. It ultimately could be perceived as an environmentally responsible, job-creating business with true concerns for downtown.

Cities and towns are complex, integrated, co-dependent systems and should be conceptualized as such to create the most synergy and financial/environmental health. A study by the Urban Land Institute (ULI) and the Coalition for Urban Transitions, supported by a consortium of leading global real estate investors and managers, shows that well-designed, compact cities are better for investors as well as citizens and the environment. According to their press release Successful Investing in Density:

> Cities with "good density"—dense development that is thoughtfully designed to promote a high quality of life—may be more resilient and prosperous in the long term. According to the report, these cities are more likely to provide higher risk -adjusted real estate investment returns than cities without "good density." It marks the first-ever study attempting to quantify the impact of quality of place on real estate investment returns.

City officials and land planners would do well to reassess a broken system that rewards waste and sprawl while reducing the tax base for desperately needed infrastructure.

New Housing Developments Incorporating Local Food Production

Real estate development and food production are not usually discussed as mutually inclusive enterprises. Each has its own unique place in our highly segmented society with virtually no crossover opportunities exploited. This narrow thinking leaves a lot of opportunities and benefits on the table. It's like a business merger where two or more companies have unique areas of specialization that can complement each other, thus creating new entities with expanded marketing/production capabilities and financial leverage. The whole is greater than the sum of the parts, as they say.

In this example, we will be merging real estate development with food production, two totally separate industries whose end users require both housing and food. Incorporating food production (small farms) into real estate development models brings a multitude of benefits and opportunities with regard to finance, health, and overall quality of life. It's maximizing ALL available assets to create more synergy and leverage. This creates added value to the development in a number of ways:

- Local food production is, for the most part, healthier, fresher, more convenient, and less expensive than supermarket food.
- It eliminates logistical problems of long food transport and its added costs.
- People are now, more than ever, concerned about the origins of their food and how it is produced. This assures residents of high-quality food.
- Small farms within the community create a more wide-open, less congested feel for residents, thus adding better views, more property value and ultimate demand.
- Food production can create additional revenue streams for the community if sold to local restaurants, farmers markets, etc.
- The fertile farm areas absorb massive amounts of storm-

Serenbe Community Garden in Georgia

water, thus minimizing the chances of flooding, and reducing the strain on already overtaxed sewer systems. It also reduces the need for the number of sewer lines found in conventional developments, which considerably reduces infrastructure costs.

The benefits are many, but this concept is nowhere to be found in mainstream real estate development. Why? This is because the construction industry is extremely slow to adapt to necessary changes, therefore leaving massive opportunities and benefits untapped. Hopefully, you will recognize the advantages of different land use designs, and profit from their implementation.

Getting back to our example, the designated farm areas will show a return on investment in the form of food sales, open space, flood/drought mitigation, and better views. The bottom-line returns from the farmland may be increased through different acquisition methods. That is to say, rather than paying for this additional land up front, it could possibly be leased, thus freeing up additional equity for other purposes. Or, a non-profit land trust can be formed, whereby the land is paid for by tax-deductible donations from people supporting environmental stewardship, local economies, health, and sustainability. The land trust can also be used to buy up more land in other areas for similar developments.

A separate land acquisition company can also be structured as a for profit business. Income can be generated by leasing or selling the farm land areas to developers or housing development managers, managing the farm for developments, selling the food to local residents or restaurants, and giving classes on food growing. All the while the land value continues to rise. It can be structured as a lease for X number of years with or without an option to buy, or a straight sale. This is one more step towards decentralization and self reliance, and thereby putting more money back into the local economy while becoming less dependent on large corporate agribusiness.

Today, there are worldwide sanctions on Russian exports, purportedly due to their invasion of Ukraine. With Russia being the world's largest supplier of fertilizer (Approximately 25% originates in Russia), many farmers are unable to grow crops, the repercussions of which are now being felt worldwide in the form of massive price increases and food shortages.

The global economic system is a house of cards ready to fall at the first major disturbance. Take one card out and the whole thing starts collapsing, as we are more or less seeing now. Industry crossover and strategic partnerships/joint ventures provide mutual benefit and create more stability, self reliance and independence, as in this case with real estate and food production

People's lives are at the mercy of psychopathic world leaders whose egos and political careers are more important to them then solving problems. In fact, war, and control over basic needs for survival just increases their power. Problems are often created so the governments can offer their own "solutions" which give them even further control. I don't mean to digress, but the point is to look at your situation in an all inclusive, synergistic way in order to remain as independent as possible from large corporate and governmental interests.

Farm Management

Let's face it, builders are not farmers, nor do they really want to be. The residents of a given community may know a little about farming, but probably not nearly enough to prepare the soil, plant, maintain, and harvest crops, That said, there is an opportunity for the landowner, be it a land trust, builder, individual, or community as a whole, to put a farm management team into place. This is an important step, as a good creative management team can make the farm areas into profitable ventures in and of themselves. All it really

Tampa Bay area home with front yard vegetable garden,

takes is one person who knows the ins and outs of farming. He/she can then hire workers from the community, or nearby, to work the farm while at the same time learning the food production business. Everyone wins.

Crops don't have to be limited to designated farm areas only. Food can be grown in fronts or backs of homes or offices in lieu of grass. People just have to expand their perceptions of what looks good, or not. Why is a symmetrically manicured lawn more acceptable than vegetable or fruit plants and trees? Is healthy food more important than a toxic, high maintenance lawn, or not? Who decided that lawns were to be the only accepted norm in new subdivisions? These are questions one needs to ask, or better yet, builders need to ask when planning a new development.

Other Benefits

Builders are subject to stringent environmental impact regulations, especially these days. Stormwater mitigation is high on the enforcement list of local municipalities, as flooding and pollution runoff can have devasting effects on communities.

In order to meet stormwater requirements, builders have to first apply for a grading permit. To do so, the builders must submit a detailed topographical map indicating potential stormwater flow volume, directions, and retention areas for overflow. The area must be graded so the stormwater flows to areas that can absorb or retain excess water while not damaging buildings or roads, etc. This is a long, expensive process as excavation and grading require additional heavy equipment and skilled operators.

Adding farm areas to a development will not only generate revenue (food sales, higher property values...), but will also absorb significant amounts of stormwater, due in part to the high organic composition of the soil. In fact, adding just 1% more organic material to soil will increase the water absorption capabilities from anywhere between 2,000 and 12,000 gallons per acre. This was explained in our recent interview with the Soil Renaissance Project.

Since adding farmland to a development significantly increases the stormwater absorption capabilities, less excavation is required for retention ponds, swales, and grading, not to mention fewer sewer lines. These are significant savings for the developer. In order to make it even more efficient, constructed wetlands could be added in and around the farm to absorb any overflow from heavy rain. These adjacent areas would also help irrigate the farmland in times of drought, thus lessening the need for more municipal water usage.

The financial, health, and environmental benefits should warrant serious consideration of farmland integration into new developments.

The Many Advantages of Sustainable Farming Methods

Once the decision has been made to include a farm into a building development, one should design it for maximum yield with minimal cost. while eliminating excess nutrient runoff.

This should make the farm more profitable and self-sufficient, thus eliminating the need for subsidies from either the builder or property owners. On the contrary, since the farms provide additional revenue streams, financial institutions may be more likely to lend money for such developments.

There are many case studies that quantify the benefits of sustainable farming, some of which will be discussed in detail later. There were several common denominators that were most influential to the success of these farms. Those were:

1) Planting Cover Crops

These are crops planted during the off season such as winter, or between cash crops. These plants add organic matter to the soil which increases water retention and infiltration, adds nutrients, reduces erosion, suppresses weeds and provides habitat for beneficial insects. They also provide a food source for predatory mites and parasitic wasps in the form of pollen and nectar. This helps control other insect pests and therefore reduces the need for pesticides. Some good cover crops include Rye, Clover, Buckwheat and some native plants. The best cover crops to use depends, of course, on the situation, climate, types of crops planted etc.

2) Non Tillage in lieu of Conventional Tillage

Conventional tillage turns the soil over and exposes it to wind and heavy rain resulting in erosion. It also makes the soil more susceptible to compaction and hardening. With no tillage, a drill or seed planter creates individual seed troughs while leaving the surrounding areas in a vegetative state, thus protecting the soil from sun exposure and erosion.

Farms as Functioning Ecosystems

Farms that provide the best yields at the lowest cost act as healthy, interconnected, symbiotic ecosystems. A complex series of cause and effect relationships results in rich, healthy, productive soil. The Lakes section discussed similar relationships, and how these chains of events produced clear, healthy lake ecosystems. Planting soil cover crops in conjunction with no-till planting enables these systems to function optimally. This is not unlike the effects littoral zone plantings in lakes have on water quality.

Cover crops and no tilling provide protective plant cover all year round which also maintains living root systems. These systems support the formation of beneficial bacteria, fungi, and other microbes which release nutrients back into the soil. Without these cover crop roots, many nutrients would be lost to surface water erosion rather than being absorbed back into the soil.

Microbial diversity and numbers are directly related to year-round planting covers. These microbes are also influential in moderating/preventing disease, harmful insects, and weeds, thus reducing the need for herbicides and pesticides. Farmland that is continuously covered with plantings is more in tune with natural systems that are inherently resilient to severe weather, disease, insects, and the like.

Housing developments that incorporate farms, and in particular these methods, should have distinct selling advantages over conventional developments. Integrating this type of farming into building models only serves to reinforce public perception of sustainability and regeneration, while lowering costs, increasing revenue streams and adding property value.

Creating Joint Ventures for Synergy and Efficiency

The real estate development industry and public works departments would do well to emulate the engineering systems and relationships found in nature. Trees, for example, are social beings, and tend to clump together where it is easier to care for one another and share nutrients. They also recognize the benefits of creating strategic relationships with other life forms, such as Mycelium fungi. The fungal threads grow on the roots in order to absorb water and nutrients there. Not only do they grow on the roots themselves, they continue to grow out well beyond the reach of the roots and bring the water and nutrients back to the roots. This creates a root system with extended range and an augmented ability to absorb water much further out than the roots themselves. That's the quid pro quo. The fungi take a little bit of the roots' water, but in return, they bring in much more due to their extended network.

Another joint venture is between the pine tree and the fungi Laccaria bicolor. These fungi release toxins that kill small organisms in and around the tree. When the organisms die and decompose, they release phosphorus back into the soil, which is beneficial fertilizer for the tree.

Becoming more localized, and less dependent on large centralized systems requires implementing techniques and strategic relationships that help local economies outperform large conglomerates. These partnerships and engineering feats abound in the natural world. One just has to look around their immediate surroundings to find them. If you look close enough, you will come to appreciate the efficacy of natural systems working in cooperation, and their ability to overcome obstacles as symbiotic partners.

Chapter Nine

Sustainable Building and Architecture

Incorporating Local Climate Data into Designs for Efficiency and Resiliency

We can not solve our problems with the same level of thinking that created them
– Albert Einstein

The previous chapters outlined many design principles that capitalized on the attributes of the surrounding landscape and water systems for more efficiency and profit. This next section will focus more on structural building designs, but always within the larger context of building and landscape operating as one synchronous unit.

As editor and publisher of White Pine—The Sustainable Real Estate Journal, I receive a plethora of press releases on new technologies designed to create more sustainability. Many are good, some not, and I applaud all those creative minds working to bring more balance, efficiency, and self-reliance into real estate. These products can be expensive to buy and install. Since it is the focus of this book to CUT costs by working synergistically with the natural world, it is important to realize ALL options BEFORE spending on new technology. Simple procedures like strategic tree placement for shade or wind mitigation, constructing raingardens or marshes to prevent flooding; the introduction of aquatic plants to restore lake ecosystems, etc., should all at least be considered.

These can all be done by you, at minimal to no cost, and with good results. It effectively uses the forces of nature to your advantage. Like a symphony orchestra, all components are playing with balance and precision, creating magnificent harmonies.

Look at your property as one living, breathing, interconnected being, with no delineation between building, land, and water. Any action should take into account its effect on the whole. Here, the whole really IS greater than the sum of the parts. Linear, disjointed thinking (as is common today) is limited in scope.

There are hundreds of cause-effect relationships going on behind the scenes. Thinking in a more integrated manner will reveal many possibilities for the built environment and the natural world to work in tandem as a complementary team. Problems are better solved using the innate, balancing forces of the entire landscape. A building will be more efficient if designed around those forces rather than against them. This runs counter to the status quo building methods where interchangeable parts and conformity dominate the industry.

Most of today's buildings, including new construction, are inefficient, obtrusive, and polluting. Granted, inroads are being made, especially with a few newer, large-scale commercial construction projects. However, from what I have seen, most residential and commercial building is still entrenched in archaic methodologies. These obsolete practices have been the norm for so many years, and has become the standard for building construction and design—a standard by which real estate is valued and marketed. As such, there is a cost to pay for any deviation from this standard.

The real estate industry just loves conformity. Take your normal residential subdivision that is less than 15 years old. Picture rows of two-story square houses, all with green lawns in front and back. Newly-planted identical-looking saplings line the street in perfect symmetry. Most homeowner association rules state that all properties should be in conformity, and fines are issued if they are not, even if the proposed changes reduce polluting stormwater runoff and flooding. Nor does it matter if the changes provide more protection from wind and noise, create more efficient thermal insulation, double roof life, or lower utility expenses. Regardless of all those benefits, conformity is not to be compromised. Some of these new construction methods will be discussed in the following pages. Then you can decide if conformity is still so important, because there is a high price to pay for it.

So, you may say, why don't you just build your own house outside of a subdivision? While that is most definitely an option, it does not address the **acceptance** of sustainable, resilient real estate in the **mainstream**. Otherwise, it will remain a fringe industry with limited impact and minimal benefits. Like everything else in this society, the construction industry is becoming more centralized, with mass-produced, interchangeable designs being imposed on diverse landscapes of all kinds; landscapes with such enormous potential if used creatively with the building process.

Conformity in and of itself stifles creativity, and society is heading more and more in this direction. The following pages will reveal designs that outperform conformity. When accepted into the mainstream economy, many of these principles will become even more cost effective due to economies of scale. Our only agenda is to see a major shift in real estate development planning and design—a transformation to where the natural world is considered a living being with equal rights to exist, and where ALL the benefits of doing so are realized.

Previous chapters discussed how nature's designs are at once complex and efficient—an efficiency the real estate industry would do well to emulate. Looking at the delivery systems of a tree would reveal a well organized, complex, interconnected web, from the root structure to the trunk, branches, and leaves. There exists an effectual network of speed and transport that is self-sustaining and renewing, with little or no waste or "collateral damage."

Architect Paolo Soleri designed buildings and cities with a major emphasis on efficiency, complexity, and "smallness," a "lean alternative" to car-dependent, sprawling suburbia. He viewed the built environment as a living, interdependent entity—land, inhabitants, buildings, vegetation and bodies of water all interacting as one complex organism.

Later in this chapter are some designs that defy conformity and the reckless, wasteful status quo. These are included to help you "think outside the box," and to establish valuable alternatives to developing and managing real estate.

Designing With Climate–An Historical Perspective

The calamity we call modern development, with all its wasteful, expensive, and destructive designs, was not always the norm. There was a movement for more integrated, climate-based architecture as early as the 1930's. Some of the most influential architects leading the way were Swiss-French Charles-Édouard Jeanneret (aka Le Corbusier), and the Hungarian-born Olgyay brothers - Victor and Aladar. Their concept was to incorporate local climate, sun angles, prevailing winds, elevation, and topographical features into their designs to create more efficient, healthier, and comfortable living spaces with less reliance on fossil fuels.

Le Corbusier used to say, "*Teach your children that architecture is about sunlight and flows.*" Victor Olgyay wrote about using shading charts, solar paths and solar azimuth angles, wind velocities and humidity in his 1963 book "Design with Climate: Bioclimatic Approach to Architectural Regionalism." The Architectural Forum magazine used to publish extensive articles on "the atmosphere as an underused resource" and how to maximize design efficiency using local climatic data.

This movement was referred to as Progressive Architectural Modernism, and was embraced by the Vargas administration in Brazil back in the 1930's. Politics aside, they had a vision of a prosperous, more independent Brazilian future with less dependency on volatile market forces—to ultimately improve living and working conditions for all citizens.

One building that best exemplifies this Architectural Modernism was the Ministry of Education and Health in Brazil, built from 1936 to 1942. The heat and glare of the sun in Brazil's hot climate make indoor cooling and shading a priority. To that end, the north-facing façade was equipped with operable louvers, all of which can be independently adjusted to different sun angles. The outer face of the louvers are heat deflecting, while the inner face is light reflecting to increase daylighting inside the building.

The Edificio Seguradoras, a Brazilian office building, constructed in 1949 for the insurance industry had similar designs, but their shading louvers were automatically controlled from the inside. There were many other similarly-designed buildings included the Northwestern Insurance (1950), and Prudential (1949) buildings in Los Angeles, CA. Some had more extensive louver systems to include both horizontal and vertical planes to account for diurnal and seasonal sun angles.

Josep Lluis Sert's American Embassy in Baghdad (built between 1955-1961) was one of the most climatically-attuned buildings. The roof was retrofitted into a habitable lush garden which not only extended roof life, but also provided excellent insulation from heat and cold, not to mention extra space it provided for meetings, eating, or just relaxing. (See the section on Living Roofs for more on living roof construction and benefits.) The shading louvers and shutters operated both horizontally and vertically, and screens were strategically placed for optimum heat diffusion and visibility.

Vietnamese American Richard Nuetra was considered a leader of architectural modernism. He was sent by the U.S. state department to exchange and promote modern architectural climatic design techniques for U.S. embassy buildings. *"An architect of tomorrow," he said, "will be an applied biologist, and this includes all the psychology that branches out from temperature and climate."* He saw the universe of which we are a part as a dynamic continuum...."*Galactic, atmospheric, biospheric, terrestrial ... molecular and subatomic interconnections and buildings' envelope as a temporary inflection or mediation of this condition."*

Architectural journals worldwide began publishing extensive articles to help with climactic architectural design. These contained sun path diagrams, wind patterns, topographical information, temperature averages, humidity. and other climate data.

In the late 1940's early 50's the Climate Control Project was created to help design buildings that conformed to landscapes as opposed to destroying landscapes to accommodate standardized designs. In his 1966 essay "The Economics of the Coming Spaceship Earth," economist Kenneth Boulding wrote about the need for an economic system that replaces run away consumption and planned obsolescence with resourcefulness and durability. His reference to earth as a limited spaceship with finite resources emphasized the need for a more efficient and integrated standard of building.

These efforts made perfect sense if the end game was to maximize efficiency, reduce costs, lesson dependency on fossil fuels, and create healthier indoor and outdoor space. There was, however, much resistance to these principles by special interest groups and corporate lobbyists who profited more from a system being completely dependent upon technology and fossil fuel—a system dominated by air conditioning and tightly sealed building envelops.

In 1959 the American Society of Refrigeration Engineers (ASRE) merged with the American Society of Heating and Air-Conditioning Engineers (ASHAE) to form the American Society of Heating, Refrigeration and Air-Conditioning Engineers (ASHRAE). This was a powerful group that looked to expand their influence and create a mechanized HVAC-dependent, unified building model that would fit any conditions, worldwide. Tall glass and steel buildings with no opening windows soon became a symbol of financial and political power.

Many architects bought into these HVAC-dependent plans, and

seemed unwilling to take on the extra complex burden of collecting, interpreting, and applying local climatic data into their designs. Many also did not like the restrictions it placed on them. That is to say, their unique designs may be compromised to account for shading, stormwater absorption, airflows, etc. Due to this lack of interest, many articles on the subject ended up in publications like Scientific American rather than mainstream architectural journals.

Then came the post-World War II "Great Acceleration," a massive geopolitical movement to create more fossil fuel-dependent infrastructure with an almost exclusive reliance on HVAC systems and standardized, tightly sealed buildings. This came as the result of political forces, economic subsidies, and industry influences which created inextricable ties between architecture and the oil economy. No surprise there. A total reliance on mechanized systems rather than shading (moveable louvers, tree shading, etc.) and other climatic solutions shortly became the norm, and was expected in all new buildings. Modern architecture embraced this technology and were complicit in its pervasiveness.

Make no mistake, the proponents of climatic design were by no means refuting the need for air conditioning. They were more interested in complimentary designs that would create a balance of technological and natural systems for more efficient performance, rather than exclusive dependence on one or the other. They considered the atmosphere an "underused resource" that should be factored into design processes to improve living and working conditions, while helping to bring about more political and economic stability. Architect Daniel Barber aptly states in his book "Modern architecture and Climate: Design Before Air Conditioning,"

> Given the preeminence of HVAC, and of the sealed façade and the fully conditioned interior, interior spaces in industrialized economies (in the United states in particular) became increasingly cut off from the environment conditions that surround

them. Architects generally saw no need to understand the principles of climate design methods, or even analysis.

Earth-Sheltered Construction

As the name implies, this is construction that is partially or completely sheltered by earth. What may come to mind with many people is that earth-sheltered construction means living underground—as in a basement. It is more like living above ground but with some walls covered by built-up dirt, leaving plenty of room for windows and skylights. Windows are strategically placed to maximize sun exposure and light penetration, while the earth sheltered walls are specifically located to insulate from noise, cold north winds, and/or baking sun.

When it comes to insulation, nothing quite compares to earth itself. It provides excellent protection from the elements, and dirt is everywhere around you. Equally important, earth-sheltered construction conforms with the existing unique landscape and with the least amount of disruption to it. There is an almost seamless blending of building and land—the merging of two distinct and separate elements into a unified, efficient structure.

The surrounding landscape is virtually unscathed, as compared to rows of obtrusive boxes indiscriminately placed on a landscape bulldozed into a flat, desolate, lifeless terrain. The innate problem-solving capabilities of these natural systems (alluded to throughout this book) are disregarded in favor of universal designs—one size fits all climates, topography, etc. The problems created by this dumbed-down, large-scale production are shouldered by the end user, the buyer—you.

Inefficient factory-style subdivisions are springing up across the country, and around the world, leveling once lush landscapes into bare patches of dirt. You can begin to change this deleterious course with your real-estate, right now.

So why consider earth-sheltered construction at all? Here are some benefits:

1) Excellent insulation from heat, cold, and noise.
2) Absorbs polluting stormwater runoff
3) Creates more wildlife habitat
4) Self-sustaining and regenerating
5) More wind resistant
6) Reduces heat island effect
7) Lowers utility costs
8) Conforms to the landscape
9) Longer life than conventional construction

Earth-sheltered construction could range anywhere from one small section of just one wall to a 100% earth sheltered building, including the entire roof and most walls covered by earth and vegetation.

Like all other techniques described in this book, earth-sheltered construction should be used for optimal efficiency based upon your unique circumstances. It may only be appropriate for just one wall or section thereof to be used. A wall facing west in a hot climate could be earth-sheltered for excellent heat insulation from the blistering afternoon sun. Conversely, northern exposed walls could be shielded from high winds and cold. The same holds true for noise reduction/elimination from busy roads (a recording studio requiring both main-road exposure and silence comes to mind), industry, loud music, or noisy neighbors. There is absolutely no better sound insulation than dirt.

Let's look at a restaurant/nightclub example. You want to open a restaurant with an adjoining nightclub. You found a great lakefront property, which would be ideal for your clientele. There would be lakeside dining for breakfast, lunch, and dinner, and live music at night. The immediate area is mixed-use zoning (residential and commercial), and across the lake is all residential. The nightclub noise would be a problem for the residents and businesses in the immediate area. Also, since sound travels extremely well across bodies of water where there are no obstructions, the music would create problems for the residents across the lake as well.

The solution to both problems would be to build the restaurant section with conventional construction, as large windows would be needed to capture the beautiful waterfront view. The excavated dirt from that building could then be used to form an earth barrier around and on top of the nightclub section. This club would be built with typical earth-sheltered construction, thus eliminating any noise problems.

There are other benefits. The shoreline would be more attractive for residents and visitors alike, since the view and would not be cluttered by a large, conventionally constructed building right on the waterfront. Instead, it would look more like a small hill covered with native vegetation. Tables could be placed there for customers to eat outside in a park-like setting. This essentially adds more restaurant capacity with no additional expense or land acquisition. The view from inside the restaurant would be better as well due to the absence of any large obstructions.

Your stormwater fees would be reduced as they are calculated on the total impervious area of your site. Earth-sheltered construction absorbs and filters stormwater, allowing less polluting runoff into the lake, thereby improving lake water quality. (See the Lakes chapter, which goes into detail about the direct correlation between water clarity and property values.) You could be, in effect, improving the water quality and thus helping to increasing property value. It also creates more wildlife habitat, and helps reduce heat island effects on those hot summer days.

Picture yourself before the local planning board trying to get the required permits for your restaurant/club. Whatever objections arise can be dealt with. In fact, you can make the case that you are improving the area for all the aforementioned reasons. You could even set a precedent for this type of construction to proliferate on the waterfront.

Some concerns about this construction include dampness (because some living area may be partly below grade), structural integrity due to the excessive weight of dirt which requires proper support, and natural lighting.

Dampness – Cool earth against warmer interior walls creates condensation, resulting in damp, musty air similar to that found in poorly insulated basements. This can be prevented by properly insulating against the cooler exterior. It is beyond the scope of this book to provide detailed construction planning, but a qualified contractor who has experience with this type of construction should be able to create buildings with bone-dry interiors.

Structural Integrity – Additional stress is placed on the load-bearing structures due to the excessive weight of dirt. A structural engineer should be consulted to ensure adequate support, not only against the final building weight, but during the construction process. Ideally, the weight will be equally distributed, but during construction, trucks may dump entire loads in one place creating more stress than planned for. Heavy machinery moving in and around the site creates additional stress on the structure. All of this needs to be taken into account.

Natural Light – Earth-sheltered construction does not preclude the use of skylights or side/front windows. Care should be taken to get the best sun exposure on the windows given your particular latitude, climate, etc.

Water – It is important to have the floor well above the water table, as water levels may rise during heavy rains. Dig a hole and find out where the water table begins, or consult a qualified hydrologist. Surface water from storm runoff should be avoided as well. Take a careful look at a topographical map and mark the water flow patterns. Try to avoid them, but if you cannot, redirect the flow away from the structure with the use of swales.

There are many problems that kill real estate transactions. An otherwise perfect property for an individual or company may be overlooked due to seemingly insurmountable obstacles. Some of those problems may be solved with partial or complete earth-sheltered construction.

The earth is alive, and solves many problems if given the chance. Working with these natural forces benefits not only property owners, but all living beings. Like it or not, our actions go far beyond property lines, as living systems know no man-made boundaries. Earth-sheltered construction is life-enhancing, and by default, will benefit the surrounding landscape. As mentioned earlier, the strength of an economy is directly proportional to the health of its ecosystems, and this is one more step in that direction.

Energy-Efficient Upgrades – A Case Study

The U.S. Department of Housing and Urban Development (HUD) conducted the following study. Energy saving upgrades were made to buildings on the Cocopah Indian reservation in Arizona, a low-lying desert region with an extremely hot, dry climate. The goal was to find the upgrades with the highest energy saving efficiencies, payback times, and investment values.

The site has three eight-unit apartment buildings and a community building, all built in 2003. Each of the 24 units is between 855 and 1,107 square feet. Given the hot climate, the largest utility expense is space cooling. Exterior window shades and low-E thermal windows were each analyzed for overall efficiency. The analysis included internal rate of return (IRR), net present value (NPR), and the number of years for the investment to pay back.

Internal rate of return (IRR) is the annual yield on a monetary investment. A project is a good investment if its IRR is greater than the rate of return that could normally be earned by an alternative investment (other projects, bonds, bank accounts, etc.). For this project, five percent is assumed as the minimum acceptable rate of return. The net present value (NPV) calculation uses a discount rate to find the present value of savings occurring over a period of future dates. This takes into account the time value of money, as money saved or earned today is worth more than at some time in the future. The discount rate is your minimum acceptable rate of return. Again, five percent is assumed.

Investments have a positive NPV when the IRR is greater than the desired rate of return, or discount rate. Therefore, projects with an IRR greater than the discount rate and a positive NPV are considered good investments and are recommended

Exterior Window Shade

Protection from the overheating effects of direct sunlight may be best accomplished by adding shading devices to the exterior of windows on the south and/or west side of the building. Using interior window shades is helpful but allows the heat to enter through the window, while exterior shades prevent some of the solar radiation from reaching the window and, therefore, entering the building.

The windows on the south side of the building had no exterior shading except for a small overhang over the second floor windows. Louvered shades were placed directly above the windows on the building's south side. This alone saved 1,860 kWh, resulting in annual cost savings of $242.

If 8' decks were added to the second floor to shade the first floor windows, 2,240 kWh could be saved annually, resulting in an annual cost savings of $291.

Exterior Window Shade Upgrade

	Annual Energy Savings		Economic Analysis			
Options	kWh	Cost	Investment	IRR	NPV	Payback
4' window shades only	1,860	$242	$2,000	10%	$1,015	8.27 yrs.
Deck and window shades	2,240	$291	$6,000	0%	-$2,373	20.62 yrs.

Triple Pane Low-E Window

The original windows of the building were typical double pane windows with clear glazing. By replacing them with triple pane window that have low emissivity, 2,100 kWh may be saved annually, resulting in an annual cost savings of $273. The lifespan of windows is calculated at 20 years. The window replacement with triple pane windows will pay back in just over the 20-year lifespan.

There are federal tax credit incentives and Arizona public services incentives also available. These would proportionally lower costs and increase investment value. They were not factored in these examples

Material, labor, and energy costs will vary over time and region, and these numbers should only be used as a general guide as to the effectiveness of each upgrade. Here, the decision to upgrade with either new windows or shade overhangs should be made quite clear. It stands to reason that the closer you get to the source of the problem, the better the efficiency—for the most part.

Window shades or overhangs block the sun before hitting the windows, whereas new windows will still take the brunt of the solar heat. Regardless of how energy efficient they are, how many panes they have, or whether they are gas-filled or not, they still will not be as efficient as simple exterior shades.

Low E Window Upgrade

Annual Energy Savings		Economic Analysis			
kWh	Cost	Investment	IRR	NPV	Payback
2,100	$237	$6,000	-1%	-$2,598	21.98 yrs.

Spray Foam Insulation

Keeping heat out of buildings in hot climates is an ongoing challenge. Some of the largest transmission of heat into buildings is through the roof. During the summer months when it is averaging 93 degrees outside, attic temperatures can be in excess of 130 degrees. This heat radiates directly into the living/working area and puts that much more strain on the HVAC system. In addition, many buildings have air conditioning ducts in the attic or crawl spaces. Cool air traveling through those ducts warms up to one extent or another, no matter how well the ducts are insulated.

Spray foam insulation helps to solve this problem at the source by insulating the roof itself, thus preventing heat from entering the attic in the first place. Rick Duncan, PhD, technical director at the Spray Polyurethane Foam Alliance says this type of insulation keeps attic areas only about five degrees warmer than the living space. Based on their studies and those of the Florida Solar Energy Center, the average energy savings from spray foam insulation is between 10% and 20% compared to conventional fiberglass insulation.

A report by engineering consultant David W. Yarbrough, PhD, compared R-values (thermal resistance) of fiberglass, open cell spray foam, and closed cell spray foam insulation. The resistance levels were measured with a heat flow meter apparatus. There are two types of foam-based insulation—open cell or closed cell. The open cell insulation is composed of air-filled cells with an R-value of approximately 3.5 per inch. The open cells absorb water and are flexible; therefore, it does not reinforce the structural integrity of the building and allows some moisture to seep through.

Closed cell insulation contains closed cells that are filled with argon or similar gasses. It is more rigid and, therefore, provides structural reinforcement to the roof. The R-value is 6.5 per inch, almost twice that of open cell insulation. Given the closed cell structure of this insulation, it is impervious to moisture and does not allow seepage into the attic area. The humidity will be somewhat similar to the living area underneath.

Costs to insulate with spray foam ranges between $1.50 and $5.00 per square foot, with the closed cell foam cost being at the high end. These costs are also dependent upon project size and location. A general rule of thumb is that spray foam costs about three times more than conventional insulation.

The above are just installation numbers. If the structure has existing insulation and you wanted it removed, the additional cost of removal is about $1.00 per square foot, if the insulation is laid over the attic floor, as it is in most cases. It would be a little more, if it were to be removed from the rafters.

Other spray foam benefits include:

- R-values do not deteriorate over time like fiberglass insulation.
- The air quality is improved due to the absence of dust and fibers from typical insulation.
- The acoustic quality is improved, as road and ambient noise from outside is absorbed more efficiently.

Foam insulation also strengthens the roof system. It is sprayed on as liquid and slowly expands into every crack and crevice, forming an almost airtight seal with no leakage. This expansion adds resistance to the rafters and roof, thus reinforcing the structural integrity.

One minor downside to foam-based insulation is since it is applied directly to the roof bed between the rafters, a tight seal is created, which pushes heat back up through the roof. This slightly increases the temperature of the outer roof surface. If conventional asphalt shingles were used, the life span of those shingles would be reduced by two years on average. Needless to say, metal or other more permanent roofs would not have this problem. Using a corrugated Styrofoam buffer between the foam insulation and the roof bed can eliminate this external heating of the roof surface. The air-filled Styrofoam insulates the roof bed from the foam insulation and eliminates any additional heating up of the shingles.

Spray foam insulation solves problems closer to the source and, as such, is typically more efficient and cost effective. If you were seriously considering using this material, it would still be advisable to consult with experts in the field.

Plumbing

Plumbing can be costly, whether for a new installation or partial revamping of an existing system. Three most widely used plumbing materials are copper, PEX (cross-linked polyethylene), and CPVC (Chlorinated Polyvinylchloride Piping), and each has its pros and cons.

Water Quality

Interior surface roughness of piping material has a direct effect on water quality, especially as it affects the growth of bacteria, parasites, fungi, viruses and other biofilm. The rougher the surface, the easier it is for organisms to attach to the pipe interior and continue to grow there.

CPVC and PEX are the smoothest materials, with consistent surface roughness of 12.1 micrometers and 13.7 micrometers respectively. (One micrometer equals 0.001 mm, or about 0.000039 inch.) New copper starts out very smooth at 7.9 micrometers, but becomes much rougher (to 2,600 micrometers) as it ages, This dramatically increases biofilm growth potential over time.

The study "Biofilm Formation Potential of Pipe Materials in Internal Installations" found Legionella bacteria in test water was considerably higher in PEX and copper than in CPVC, due in part to surface roughness differences.

Durability

PEX is more susceptible to degradation from chlorine typically found in municipal water supplies. To counter that problem, antioxidants are added to PEX in the manufacturing process, but these are gradually used up and eventually lose effectiveness. If you use well water, that is obviously not a problem. CPVC on the other hand, is much more resistant to chlorine oxidizers and require no additional antioxidants. Over time, copper is subject to mineral buildup and corrosion from various elements in water supplies, including but not limited to chlorine. This can eventually lead to pinhole leaks and biofilm buildup.

Both PEX and CPVC will degrade if exposed to ultraviolet radiation, so they should not be used outdoors in direct contact with sunlight. This is not an issue with copper. However, given its rigidity copper can rupture if water starts to freeze in the lines. The flexibility of PEX, and to a somewhat lesser degree CPVC, enables them to expand and contract more easily, therefore preventing bursting pipes.

Cost

Copper is by far the most expensive in terms of material and installation cost. The material cost of PEX and CPVC are close in price and significantly lower than copper. The installation cost of PEX is lowest due mainly to its flexibility. This flexibility drastically eliminates installation costs by up to 20 percent. In many cases, one continuous length of pipe can be used without cutting and fittings since it can bend around 90 degree corners. A recent study by the National Association of Homebuilders Research Center concluded that installation costs associated with PEX plumbing saved an average of 16 man hours when retrofitting an entire home.

Living Green Roofs and Walls

Green roofs are natural, living landscapes planted on roof surfaces. This takes ugly, unproductive, and inefficient asphalt rooftops and turns them into self-renewing, highly insulated surfaces. In many cases, they add to the leasable area of a commercial building—in effect turning a hot, black surface into a rooftop café, garden, or some other type of area that complements the building's primary business.

German landscape architect Harry Maasz envisioned cities where "man will stroll from roof garden to roof garden, which will continuously crown the tops of our cities as sunlit and flowering paradises." This was in the 1930s. In the 1980s, living, or green roofs were mandated in Stuttgart, Germany, to reduce city temperatures and groundwater pollution. Since then, there were approximately 4.8 square miles of green roofs built each year in Germany.

There is nothing really new about green roofs. It's just that the gross inefficiencies of current roofing systems are becoming more obvious in a world that is embracing a more sustainable living standard. They have been around a long time. Wine and beer cellars throughout Europe used living roofs to better control temperatures. Grasses planted on rooftops in African villages help moderate the searing heat. Grass roofs have been built for centuries in northern areas like Iceland and Scandinavia as protection from extreme cold.

The city of Basel, Switzerland initiated a green roof campaign in 1997 to help mitigate the effects of extreme climate in the region, as well as increase biodiversity, save energy, and reduce flooding and water runoff problems. This was partially subsidized by an energy tax, which was voted on by the local residents. In 2006, approximately 1,711 extensive and 218 intensive (intensive typically means the substrate, or planting medium is deeper, allowing for a more diverse set of plants and provides better insulation) roofs were constructed. In 2008, roughly 23% of the flat rooftop area in Basel was green. This amounted to 3.1 gigawatt-hours of energy savings per year , according to the 2008 report, *From Pilot to Mainstream: Green Roofs in Basel, Switzerland.*

City planners and managers would do well to look at green roofs as a means to enrich the quality of life while, at the same time, making a good return on investment. The first thing to do is look at all your resources at hand and determine how to use them most effectively in solving problems.

Some Green Roof Benefits:

1) Longer roof life – a typical asphalt roof lasts approximately 15–20 years where the living roof lasts 30–50 years. Doubling the roof life also means eliminating half the waste from old torn out roofs. This significantly reduces the 6–9 million annual tons of discarded roofing material in the United States alone. (Cavanaugh 2008)

2) Better insulation – the additional layers of growing medium and plants provide extra insulation from direct sun and temperature fluctuations, which are the primary causes of roof deterioration.

3) Regenerating – rooftop plants continue to grow and propagate while requiring little to no maintenance, thereby providing additional protection over time. This is unlike a conventional roof which rapidly depreciates in value and performance.

4) Stormwater runoff reduction and filtering – A three to four inch growing medium is normally recommended for the Mid Atlantic and Great Lakes states. This usually absorbs approximately 80% of rainwater during a heavy rainstorm. The city of Chicago's sustainable development project counts green roofs in the percentage of pervious area for a given property in the calculation of stormwater retention requirements, thus reducing stormwater costs. According to a Howard University study, in order for runoff from green roofs to occur at all, rain storms generally have to accumu–

late more than one inch of water in a 24-hour period.

5) Cools surrounding air and reduces the heat island effect.

6) Reduces noise levels as a direct result of increased insulation. This could be the difference between a profitable building or not, as noise reduction increases the field of potential tenants that require quiet spaces—recording studios, libraries, nursing facilities, and residential neighborhoods.

7) Dust filtration – Just open an apartment building window in a major city and within a few hours there will be an accumulation of dust and soot on your tables. Green roofs reduce this effect.

8) Wildlife habitat – increases biodiversity in the area.

9) Protection of water supplies. More stormwater absorption reduces flooding and sewer overflows. The American Society of Landscape Architects (ASLA) studied the stormwater overflow problem in the U.S. and how green, living rooftops can significantly help reduce stormwater runoff.

> The rapid transport of water away from the built environment to natural water bodies has been an engineering problem for the past 130 years, and combined sewer systems were initially used as a cost-effective means of transporting sewage and stormwater together. With wide-scale application of municipal wastewater treatment in the mid-twentieth century, flow rate limitations of treatment plants made it very difficult to accommodate peak flows from the combined sewer systems that directed wastewater to them.
>
> Today, combined sewer systems remain in 746 municipalities in 31 states and the District of Columbia and discharge (into the local rivers, lakes, bays, and oceans) an estimated 850 billion gallons of stormwater and wastewater annually.

The green roof on the American Society of Landscape Architects (ASLA) headquarters in Washington D.C. retained approximately three quarters of the total rainfall volume falling on it over the ten-month period that data was collected.

The Greater Manchester Green Roof Program Feasibility Study documented green roof performance in Germany and Canada. The cooling requirements of two identical houses in Canada were studied—one used as a reference and the other with a green roof. The average daily summer demand for the reference house was between 6 and 8 kWh. The average demand for the green roof house was less than 2 kWh—a 66-75% reduction in cooling costs. The study then documented winter heating costs of flat roof buildings in Germany. Winter fuel bills were reduced between 3 and 10%—a maximum savings of 6.8 kWh/square meter and a minimum savings of 2 kWh per square meter.

Green roofs also enhance solar panel performance. Solar voltaic power ratings are tested under optimal conditions at 25 degrees Celsius. There is a steady decrease in panel efficiency and power output as temperatures increase over 25 degrees (see Solar Energy chapter), starting with an approximate .5% decrease in power output for every degree over 25 degrees Celsius. Performance steadily declines until there is an approximate 1.1% loss in power output for every degree over 42 degrees Celsius. Again, it is usually not one or the other, but rather an optimal combination of all options to get maximum synergy, efficiency, and return on investment.

An often overlooked benefit of green roofs is their acoustical benefits. A study done at the British Columbia Institute of Technology tested the sound insulation characteristics of vegetative sedum mats compared with traditional roofing. The average attenuation of low frequencies improved by 10 decibels with the living roofs, while the average high frequency attenuation was 30 decibels.

Other More Subjective Financial Benefits

Looking at the larger picture may help with investment decisions about green roofs, as there are other things to consider which will affect the bottom line.

Higher Property Values

Commercial properties are valued based on their net operating income. Green roofs can increase income and reduce expenses in the following ways:

1) Green roofs increase leasable area by turning rooftops into lush, park-like settings for meetings, cafes, exercise areas, etc. This additional space can increase rental income, not only for the roof top, but for the entire building.
2) Higher tenant retention as a result of these amenities
3) Lower utility costs, including stormwater fees, heating, and cooling
4) Longer roof life

Community Benefits

1) Better air quality
2) Less heat island effect
3) More biodiversity
4) Less municipal money spent on stormwater/sewer infrastructure (installation, replacement and maintenance)

The United States General Services Administration quantified the financial benefits of green roofs in their report *The Benefits and Challenges of Green Roofs On Public and Commercial Buildings*. They studied the initial investment of installing and maintaining a green roof on 5,000, 10,000, and 50,000-square foot roof surfaces in the Washington D.C. area. They then factored in only the reduced utility expenses, extended roof life, and decreased stormwater/sewer infrastructure expenditures. The 10,000-square-foot roof had a 220% return on investment, a payback of 6.4 years, and a 5% internal rate

Green living roof at the Museum of Science and Industry Tampa, FL

of return. The profitability improved as the roof sizes increased, due in part to economies of scale.

Green roofs are slow to catch on in the United States as compared to Germany, for a number of reasons—mis-information, lack of standardization, and fear of potential leaks (Weiler and Scholz-Barth 2009). The truth is that if the real benefits are outlined, quantified, and backed up with documentation, the market penetration of these roofs may increase exponentially in the U.S.

There are some bright spots in the United States. The Chicago Sustainable Development Policy includes green roofs as pervious area in the overall calculation of stormwater retention requirements. Green roofs which are also accessible to people, are credited as open space, and, therefore, reduce the open space impact fees on multi-family projects.

The Philadelphia Electric Company constructed a 45,000-square foot living roof—the largest in Pennsylvania. In 2009 the city of Toronto required a percentage of roof vegetation for large new construction projects. Eligible green roof projects for commercial, industrial, and institutional buildings also received financial incentives of $50 per square meter up to a maximum of $100,000.

Insurance companies, known for their actuarial conservatism, are also realizing the potential of sustainable design, and green, living roof systems, and are developing new programs to cover them. According to Steve Bushnell, Senior director of commercial insurance for Fireman's Fund Insurance Company, "We do business now in a way to make a profit and not jeopardize the world, our company, or the people in it."

Green Roof Construction

The following are general guidelines and points to remember when considering green roof construction. It is, however, important to consult with qualified engineers and contractors before starting such a project.

Insurance company Factory Mutual Globe recommends calculating the dead load of a completely saturated living roof at no less than 100 lbs. per cubic foot. The National Roofing Contractors Association recommends a 215 mil (.215", 5.375mm) minimum thickness of fabric -reinforced, hot fluid-applied, polymer-modified asphalt membrane (Graham 2007) to eliminate risk of leaks.

Green Roof Vegetation

The workhorse of roof surface vegetation is the sedum (over 500 species are known to date), as they most readily adapt to the harsh rooftop conditions and are somewhat unique in that they:

1) Survive in arid climates, due in part to a unique form of photosynthesis called Crassulacean Acid Metabolism (CAM). Plant pores remain closed during the day and open at night. This reduces the evaporation during hot days, while the CO2

intake occurs at night, in cooler, damper conditions.

2) Sedums have minimal, shallow root systems which are ideal for rooftops with restricted growing mediums.
3) They contain large vacuoles to store water over long periods, thus helping stabilize rooftop water runoff while increasing their the ability to withstand drought.

Growing Medium

Deeper substrates are required if the intention is to also create wildlife habitat. Growing mediums deeper than 6 inches are important for invertebrates such as beetles and spiders, as they freeze in thinner depths. A more varied plant mixture can also be used as the deeper dirt protects from extreme heat and cold. A depth of 3–4

Rooftop of the American Society of Landscape Architects building in Washington D.C.

inches is normally used in the Mid Atlantic, Great Lakes, and New England states. For hotter, drier climates, a deeper substrate is required, usually around 6 inches.

Soil for living roofs should be relatively light weight, coarse and permeable, and able to absorb large quantities of water. Pumice from volcanoes is often used, as it meets these criteria and is only 40 pounds per cubic foot when dry.

Some Green Roof Components of the ASLA (American Society of Landscape Architects) building in Washington D.C.

1) Waterproofing – Gypsum board coated with hot rubberized asphalt and fabric reinforcement was placed on the roof deck. The asphalt was applied in two coats, with a total coating thickness of about ¼ inch.

2) Root Barrier – This prevents roots from damaging the waterproofing and creating leaks. Eight inch sheets of rubberized asphalt were reinforced with polyester and then treated with root-repelling agents. The sheets were rolled onto the waterproofing while still hot so it would become embedded into it.

3) Insulation – Water resistant, high strength polystyrene boards were laid on top of the waterproofing to protect from extreme heat and cold.

4) Aeration and Drainage Mat – This created a 1/4 inch airspace to increases air flow and dry out the insulation in the event some water dripped down from the water retention mat.

5) Water Retention and Drainage Mat – This 1 inch mat was placed over the aeration mat to insure all water flowing down from the substrate would be captured or drained. It had an egg crate-shaped design. Plant roots tap into the cups for a steady supply of water. Once the cups are filled, they overflow into drainage pipes.

6) Filter Fabric – This separated the growing medium from the drainage layer.

Pervious Concrete
Reduce/eliminate flooding while recharging aquifers

Pervious concrete is porous concrete which absorbs stormwater rather than having it run-off into sewer systems, and create flooding/ pollution problems "downstream." It is made with Portland cement, washed gravel, fly ash and water, and typically has a void content of between 15 and 25 percent, which allows water to infiltrate through the pavement and into the ground below. Permeable pavement has many advantages and benefits:

1) **Lower Overall Costs and Flood Prevention**
Less than 1% of rainfall landing on a conventional concrete/ asphalt surfaces is absorbed, with about 99% of it washing onto the street. Conversely, almost 100% of rainfall landing on pervious cement is absorbed directly into the concrete and exfiltrated into the underlying soil, if designed properly. In many cases, the pavement can absorb additional stormwater from adjacent areas like lawns and rooftops, depending on the design, soil types, etc. This significantly reduces stormwater runoff from a property. While pervious pavement is slightly more expensive than traditional concrete, that extra cost pays for itself many times over by eliminating or reducing the need for additional stormwater infrastructure such as piping, excavation, sewer hook-ups, retention ponds, etc.

2) **Reduced Pollution**
Contaminated surface runoff containing things such as oil, pesticides, nutrients from fertilizers, raw sewage, agricultural runoff, etc. ends up either draining directly into waterways or through

sewer systems. If the sewer systems get overloaded, raw sewage could be released directly into the environment. This occurs on a regular basis during rainy seasons, especially where sewer infrastructure is old and in need of repair and/or expansion, which is the case more often than not. Permeable concrete significantly reduces stormwater runoff, thus lessening or eliminating toxic overflows.

3) **Aquifer Recharging**
   Land in pre-development states such as woods, meadows, marshland, etc. naturally absorbs heavy or prolonged periods of rain directly into the ground. This eventually seeps down and recharges underground aquifers. Permeable concrete essentially mimics these natural processes by absorbing surface rainwater into aquifers.

4) **Better Land Utilization**
   Building developments that do not implement pervious concrete and other stormwater reduction methods will invariably need additional land set aside for drainage ditches, retention ponds, sewer lines, etc. Land is not cheap, and that land that can be put to better use, resulting in economic and/or environmental benefit.

Designing Pervious Concrete Projects

There are many variables that go into calculating the best pervious pavement design. The following will illustrate design options in real-world scenarios.

Example 1: The subject property is a residential home in a typical subdivision located in Tampa, FL with front and back lawns, sidewalks, and a 3-car driveway. There is significant flooding in the area when a 24-hour rainfall exceeds 8 inches. The goal here is to reduce 100% of the stormwater runoff from driveways in order to help eliminate neighborhood flooding during these types of rain events.

Here are some variables that need to be taken into consideration to get maximum effects for a particular location.

Porosity

Pervious concrete is less dense than conventional concrete which allows water to filter through it. This increased porosity weakens the concrete, so the best density will depend upon the use. For driveways, 20% porosity is more than adequate, assuming the proper concrete thickness. Heavily-travelled roads, for example, would require higher strength concrete with lower porosity.

Thickness

To compensate for reduced strength, pervious concrete in this example should be approximately 5 inches, compared to 3-4 inches required for conventional concrete.

Gravel Base

This gravel layer just beneath the concrete provides additional water storage capacity until it is eventually exfiltrated down into the soil below. According to the Ready Mix Concrete Association, standard rule of thumb calls for this gravel to have 40% porosity. It is also recommended that this base be at least 1 foot above the water table. Several scenarios shown later will indicate the effects gravel base depth and porosity has on stormwater runoff.

Exfiltration rate for different soil types

Exfiltration rates are the speeds at which water is absorbed into the underlying soil, depending on the soil type. Soil types are broken down into four major categories:

A – sand or loamy sand
B – silt loam, loam
C – sandy clay loam,
D - clay, silty clay loam, clay, sandy clay

Soil type A has the fastest exfiltration rate. The rates get progressively slower with D being the slowest. This is mostly due to the larger clay content.

Average exfiltration rates for the different categories are:

A – 1-2 inches per hour
B – .5 to 1 inch per hour
C – .15 to .25 inches per hour
D – less than .1 inches per hour

Bear in mind that in order to get the most accurate rates for your particular area you should consult with an engineer, as the percentage composition of sand, silt, clay, etc. may vary.

Surface area

In this case we are looking only at the 3-car driveway which is 26 feet by 35 feet, or 910 square feet.

Now we can run various scenarios through a simulation spreadsheet designed by the National Ready Mix Concrete Association. This first example is for a 910 square foot driveway in Tampa, FL which has predominately sandy soil, with an exfiltration/absorption rate of 2 inches per hour. The precipitation volume is for a 10-year rain event for the area totaling 8.16 in. in a 24-hour period. The concrete driveway was designed as follows:

Design Parameters

Pervious Concrete	
Thickness	5 in.
Surface area	910 sq. ft.
Porosity	20%
Gravel Base	
Thickness	6 in.
Porosity	40%

Exfiltration Rate	2 in./hour
24-hour precipitation	8.16in.

This scenario creates 619 cubic feet of water for the driveway alone for a 10-year rain event of 8.16 inches within a 24-hour period. This equals 2,315,060 gallons for a typical 500-home subdivision.

All or most of this stormwater could be absorbed back into the underground aquifers rather than flooding sewer systems.

Results:

Total drained surface area:	910 sq. ft.
Storage capacity of pervious concrete	76 cubic feet
Storage capacity of gravel base	182 cubic feet
Total stormwater storage	258 cubic feet
Total precipitation volume	619 cubic feet
Five-day exfiltration volume	619 cubic feet
Total stormwater overflow	0 cubic feet
Water stored after 5 days	0 cubic feet

(1 cubic foot {1 ft^3} = 7.48 US gallons)

Now we will change the parameters by decreasing the depth of the gravel base from 6 inches to 3 inches.

Design Parameters

Pervious Concrete	
Thickness	5 in.
Surface area	910 sq. ft.
Porosity	20%
Gravel Base	
Thickness	3 in.
Porosity	40%
Exfiltration Rate	2 in./hour
24-hour precipitation	8.16in.

Results:

Total drained surface area:	910 sq. ft.
Storage capacity of pervious concrete	76 cubic feet
Storage capacity of gravel base	91 cubic feet
Total stormwater storage	167 cubic feet
Total precipitation volume	619 cubic feet
Five-day exfiltration volume	619 cubic feet
Total stormwater overflow	0 cubic feet
Water stored after 5 days	0 cubic feet

Again, all of the stormwater is still absorbed even with less gravel base.

Now we will change the exfiltration/absorption rate to .25 inches per hour to account for the possibility of a denser, more clay like soil. All other parameters remain the same.

Design Parameters

Pervious Concrete	
Thickness	5 in.
Surface area	910 sq. ft.
Porosity	20%
Gravel Base	
Thickness	3 in.
Porosity	40%
Exfiltration Rate	.25 in./hour
24-hour precipitation	8.16in.

Results:

Total drained surface area:	910 sq. ft.
Storage capacity of pervious concrete	76 cubic feet
Storage capacity of gravel base	91 cubic feet
Total stormwater storage	167 cubic feet
Total precipitation volume	619 cubic feet

Five-day exfiltration volume	461 cubic feet
Total stormwater overflow	158 cubic feet
Water stored after 5 days	0 cubic feet

Notice here, due to the different soil type, the water does not drain as well, creating an overflow of 158 cubic feet. That is still much better than the total precipitation volume of 619 cubic feet or stormwater that would run off into the street with conventional concrete.

Now we will make one more change to this last example by increasing the gravel base to the original thickness of 6 inches and see the results.

Design Parameters

Pervious Concrete	
Thickness	5 in.
Surface area	910 sq. ft.
Porosity	20%
Gravel Base	
Thickness	6 in.
Porosity	40%
Exfiltration Rate	.25 in./hour
24-hour precipitation	8.16in.

Results:

Total drained surface area:	910 sq. ft.
Storage capacity of pervious concrete	76 cubic feet
Storage capacity of gravel base	182 cubic feet
Total stormwater storage	258 cubic feet
Total precipitation volume	619 cubic feet
Five-day exfiltration volume	552 cubic feet
Total stormwater overflow	67 cubic feet
Water stored after 5 days	0 cubic feet

The 3-inch difference in gravel base reduced the stormwater overflow from 158 cubic feet to 67 cubic feet, all else being equal. As you can see, permeable concrete can be customized to get optimal, cost effective results for your situation. Climate, soil type, topography, amount of development in the surrounding areas, drainage... are all factors to consider when designing pervious concrete projects.

It is worth repeating that you should get the advice of a qualified engineer to ascertain the soil types and drainage capabilities on your property and surrounding areas, This will help you to make more accurate design parameters.

The use of pervious concrete is an efficient and effective method to solve or mitigate flooding issues. Total reliance on centralized, outdated municipal sewer systems has been shown to fail time and again. It is best to address problems at the source, in this case, the impervious surface areas of building sites—residential, commercial, industrial or whatever. These are the starting points of stormwater flow.

The previous example saved over 2 million gallons of potential stormwater from entering the streets and sewer systems, while letting it absorb back into the ground and aquifers. This was just for the driveways in one subdivision over a 24-hour period.

Today there is a major water crisis in the mid and western United States. Farmers are dependent upon pumping underground aquifers for crop irrigation. After decades of unsustainable pumping, the water levels of these aquifers have dropped drastically, making it nearly impossible for many farmers to continue crop production.

Pervious pavement combined with other stormwater management solutions, explained earlier, helps solve flooding, pollution, and aquifer depletion at once. That's a lot of bang for the buck. It also does not rely on politicians and special interest groups to implement solutions, many of whom are corrupt, . This can be done by property owners and managers themselves, in the spirit of self-reliance and independence.

Chapter Ten

Solar Energy Economics

Derate Factors and Other Decision Making Criteria

> We are like tenant farmers chopping down the fence around our house for fuel when we should be using nature's inexhaustible sources of energy
> – Thomas Edison

To some people, solar is the end-all solution to today's energy problems, while to others it is too expensive, inefficient, and with too long payback periods. This section will show there are many variables that need to be taken into account before jumping into a solar power investment—and which change depending on property type, climate, vegetation, utility prices, incentives, orientation, shading, etc., all of which affect financial viability and efficiency..

Other influences that need to be considered are known as derate factors, and their effect on the **actual** power output of PV panels, after converting sun energy into DC (direct current) power, and then to AC (alternating current) power used in buildings. These reduce the overall efficiency of solar systems and need to be considered when sizing, specifying and analyzing the benefits of solar for your situation. The following system derate factors need to be taken into account in order to get the usable power output.

1) **PV Panel Rating: -5%**
   Manufacturers rate their panels' output in terms of DC watts produced under their ideal test conditions. This is typically overvalued and the standard adjustment for this is 5%.
2) **Heat: -9%**
   Standard test conditions are normally done at or around 25 degrees Celsius, which is best for optimal PV panel performance. PV efficiency is inversely proportional to temperature increases above a certain point. As temperatures rise above 25 degrees Celsius, the PV output decreases. The panels are also affected from the heat radiation emitted from the roof surface, which can be much higher than the ambient temperature outside. If you are installing a system in a hot climate, a slightly lower output should be expected and accounted for. A United Kingdom study revealed an output decrease of 1.1% for every degree increase over 42 degrees Celsius (107 degrees Fahrenheit). Another study in Nigeria showed similar results. Both studies took into account the additional heat, approximately 20 degrees, radiating from the roof, meaning that the ambient temperatures were some 20 degrees lower than the actual panel temperature, or around 87 degrees Fahrenheit. Heat will be a factor in this example as it is in subtropical Southwest Florida.
3) **Inverter and Transformer Loss: -4%**
   The efficiency at which a typical inverter converts DC to AC is .96, a 4% loss.
4) **Dirt and debris: -5%**
   Losses due to dirt and foreign objects collecting on the PV panels blocks out some solar radiation. Areas with high pollution and minimal rainfall are affected more. In our example, the average loss is approximately a 5% .

5) **Wiring losses: -2%**
   DC wiring losses account for any electrical resistance losses in the wiring between the panels themselves, and from the panels to the inverter. AC wiring losses also take into account resistance losses from the inverter to the local utility connection.
6) **Diodes and Connections: -.5%**
   Losses from voltage drops across diodes used to block the reverse flow of current and from resistive losses in electrical connections.
7) **Shading: -1%**
   All shading is normally accounted for when determining sun hours via the software and charts previously mentioned. However, some other shading may occur such as PV panels in close proximity blocking sun on adjacent panels. A default value of 1% is normally applied when there is adequate space between rows of panels. This example assumes good spacing, therefore, -1% is applied.
8) **Tracking: -6%**
   Solar panels perform optimally when positioned at a 90-degree angle to the sun. This positioning is called altitude, or declination, and is directly related to the height of the sun in the sky. This vertical angle can be accurately measured from the date and latitude of the location. The position of the sun relative to true north as it changes during the day is called azimuth, or hour angle. It moves 180 degrees in 12 hours. Automatic tracking systems get the optimal panel positioning relative to the sun. These can be either 1- or 2-axis systems. A 1-axis system follows the azimuth alone, while a 2-axis system follows both azimuth and altitude and is the most efficient for maximizing the sun's radiation. This example assumes a standard fixed system with no automatic tracking adjustment. The derate factor for a fixed tracking system is

approximately -6 percent.

9) **Mismatch: -1.5%**
Current and voltage characteristics between panels may vary slightly due to minor manufacturing imperfections.

10) **Light-Induced Degradation: -1%**
Photovoltaic cells have a slight drop off in efficiency during the first few months of operation due to initial light exposure.

The total derate value is 35%. This is the percentage that should be **deducted** from the panel rating to give you the most accurate power output. This value will be factored into our example below.

Sizing a Residential Solar Electric System

The average daily electric use for a typical home in Tampa, Florida, is approximately 28 kilowatt hours per day. Tampa is being used as an example for several reasons. First, since there is such an abundance of sun in Florida, one would think solar electric would be at least as prevalent there as in cold-climate states such as New York, but that is not always the case.

The fact is, Florida lags behind northern states like New York, New Jersey, and Colorado in terms of total solar electric power generated. One of the main reasons is most probably the relatively low cost of electricity in Florida, which burns inexpensive coal for most of the state's electric generation. The underlying assumption is that it does not pay to install solar in areas that burn cheap coal for electricity because the payback period would be many years down the road, and the return on investment would be less than many other investment options.

Solar development in states like Florida also fall short because of the unavailability of state financial incentives. Florida's solar incentive was a rebate of $4 per watt produced, but is no longer available, at least for now. That said, this example will not include any rebates from the state, in order to keep this a conservative analysis..

The following example will demonstrate the financial viability of solar in low-cost, coal-burning states such as Florida and with no state incentives. We will be sizing a system that covers 100% of the electric requirements of a home using an average of 28 kilowatt hours per day, and assuming the occupant to be in the middle income tax bracket of 24 percent. This will later be used to determine interest rate deductions on the financing costs of the system.

The first step is to find the peak sun hours per day for your region. This area has 5.67 hours per day. Solar irradiance charts are readily available on the web, from sites such as PV Watts. There are also devices such as Solar Pathfinder, or the Solmetric Suneye, which automatically calculates sun hours based on the site's latitude and longitude coordinates. There is also a glass bubble (Suneye), which takes a 180 degree view of the site from the actual rooftop, or wherever the panel will be placed. Any obstructions that may shade parts of the panels at specific times during the day can be seen from the "eye." This is calculated into the overall sun hours per day result.

These shading results are critical to sizing a PV system. Shading on a single cell can stop the current on an entire string of PV panels. Only 20% shade can reduce power by some 40% or more in systems with conventional panel wiring. If shading is a problem, module level electronics should be used. These confine power loss to only the shaded modules.

In order to get 100% of the electricity for this home, the average daily electric use of 28 kilowatts is divided by the sun hours per day for this location: 28,000 watts/5.67sun hours = 4,938 watts, rounded up to a 5 kW system.

In order to find the number of solar panels required to generate this power, the total AC watts is divided by the **actual** solar panel rated output, which is the panel's rating less the derate factor of 35%, which was explained above. In this case, we are using 250 watt rated panels. We multiply 250 times .65 (100 minus .35) which equals a derated panel rating of 162.5. The total power output requirement of 5000 watts divided by the derated panel rating of 162.5 equals a total of 30.77, or 31 panels needed.

Now, if you think I am being overly conservative, let's do it with a derate factor of 25% rather than 35%. So, 250 times .75 equals a derated panel rating of 187.5. The output requirement of 5,000 watts divided by 187.5 equals 26.67, or 28 panels needed.

According to the U.S. Department of Energy the country average installed cost of solar electric systems is approximately $3.00 per watt. Please bear in mind that as this book is being written the advances in solar technology will be bringing this cost down over the years. So, you might say this analysis is a worst case scenario and will probably improve over time.

The 5 kW system at $3.00 per watt equals a total installed cost of $15,000. The next step is to compare the financing costs to the energy savings per month. In this area, the current electric costs are .13 per kWh and, as mentioned, an average 28kWh are needed per day. Therefore, 28 kWh X 30 days = 840 kWh per month X .13 = $109 saved per month on electric costs.

The following spread sheet breaks down the cash flow from year to year. The loan to finance the system has an interest rate of 3% over 25 years. The Federal incentive plan now has a straight credit of 24% of the total installed cost for solar water heaters, solar panels, geothermal heat pumps, and wind energy systems, with no upper limit cap. This includes all supplies and installation costs. The current law defines installation costs as "labor costs properly allocable to the onsite preparation, assembly, or original installation of the property, and for piping or wiring to interconnect such property to the home." This all boils down to a tax credit of $3,600 (.24 X $15,000) in our example. This is a tax credit, meaning you can only use it to reduce your federal income tax liability, It is not a direct cash payment. And yes, it can be rolled over to the following year in the event you cannot use it all up in the first year.

Solar Financial Analysis with 100% Financing

System Information
System Cost@ $3 per watt $15,000
Current Energy Cost $.13/kWh
Monthly Electric Usage $109
Monthly Payment $71.13

Loan Information
Interest Rate 3%
Loan Duration 25 yrs.
Loan Amount $15,000

Year	Loan Payment	Fuel Indices	Energy Savings	Tax Credit	Maintenance/ Efficiency Loss	Annual Savings (Cash Flow)
1	-853.56		1,308.00	3,600		$4,054
2	-853.56	1.10	1,438.80			585
3	-853.56	1.12	1,464.96			611
4	-853.56	1.14	1,491.12		-100	538
5	-853.56	1.16	1,517.28		-100	564
6	-853.56	1.18	1,543.44		-100	590
7	-853.56	1.21	1,582.68		-100	629
8	-853.56	1.25	1,635.00		-100	681
9	-853.56	1.29	1,687.32		-100	734
10	-853.56	1.32	1,726.56		-100	773
11	-853.56	1.37	1,791.96		-100	838
12	-853.56	1.41	1,844.28		-100	891
13	-853.56	1.45	1,896.60		-100	943
14	-853.56	1.50	1,962.00		-100	1,008
15	-853.56	1.54	2,014.32		-100	1,061
16	-853.56	1.59	2,079.72		-100	1,126
17	-853.56	1.64	2,145.12		-100	1,192
18	-853.56	1.69	2,210.52		-100	1,257
19	-853.56	1.74	2,275.92		-200	1,222
20	-853.56	1.80	2,354.40		-220	1,281
21	-853.56	1.86	2,432.88		-220	1,359
22	-853.56	1.91	2,498.28		-220	1,425
23	-853.56	1.97	2,576.76		-220	1,503
24	-853.56	2.04	2,668.32		-220	1,595
25	-853.56	2.10	2,746.80		-220	1,673

Figure 1 Solar Financial Analysis

The chart indicates there is a positive cash flow throughout the entire life of the system, but this is under the assumption there are optimal conditions of full sun every day. It also does not take into account energy use at night, where there is no solar output. This means you will have to rely on the electric grid during these times. Net metering helps to defray a lot of these costs by allowing you to sell your unused power generated during the day back to the utility, This program is not available in all states, so you should definitely check the availability of net metering in your area.

The only way to get 100% electricity at night and during dark days without reliance on the grid, is to have battery backup. That gets a bit expensive, but worth it if you want to remain completely independent of the grid.

The Appraised Values of Energy Efficient Real Estate

America is a mobile society, as most people in this country change households approximately every 5 years. The question then becomes, is it worth the trouble and expense of installing a solar system if the current residents may move in 5 or 6 years. Conventional thinking sees the payback as being much longer than 6 years and, as a result, it may be seen as a bad investment that loses money. Looking at solar energy as an investment, the rationale is that **the cost of the renewable energy installation should be less than the present value of the future energy savings for the life of the system**. That is to say, what would the accumulated energy savings from the solar system be worth today, taking into account what you could earn if you invested that money elsewhere.

The discount rate, or rate of return, used to arrive at this figure would be the after-tax mortgage interest rate on the property. This is the general method used in the appraisal world. The discount rate is lowered to reflect the tax savings or interest deduction on the loan.

Let's assume a mortgage interest rate of 3%, with the owner in the middle 24% tax bracket. The after-tax mortgage interest rate

Present Value Cash Flows With 100% Financing

Discount Rate: 2.3%

Year	Cash Flow	Factor	Present Value Cash Flow
1	4,354	0.9775	4,257
2	585	0.9555	559
3	611	0.9341	571
4	538	0.9131	491
5	564	0.8925	503
6	590	0.8725	515
7	629	0.8528	537
8	681	0.8337	568
9	734	0.8149	598
10	773	0.7966	616
11	838	0.7787	653
12	891	0.7612	678
13	943	0.7441	702
14	1,008	0.7273	733
15	1,061	0.7110	754
16	1,126	0.6950	783
17	1,192	0.6794	810
18	1,257	0.6641	835
19	1,222	0.6492	794
20	1,281	0.6346	813
21	1,359	0.6203	843
22	1,425	0.6064	864
23	1,503	0.5927	891
24	1,595	0.5794	924
25	1,673	0.5664	948
Total	**28,434**		**21,237**

Figure 2 Present Value Cash Flows

would be approximately 2.3 percent. (1 minus tax bracket of .24 equals .76. This multiplied by the mortgage rate of 3% equals 2.3%)

Figure 2 shows the present value of future energy savings to be $21,237 after 25 years, with a $15,000 installation cost. The present value of future savings would be $6,237 more than the cost of the installation. In this scenario, solar would be a good investment. In other words, if you were guaranteed a 3% return on another investment, this solar project would yield an additional $6,237 over and above the 3% return.

The numbers shown here are somewhat conservative, since photovoltaic prices are coming down as this book is being written. The projected fuel/electricity costs were taken from the U.S. Department of Energy's fuel indices, which, in my opinion, are rather conservative given the volatile political and social factors that directly affect these prices.

The previous financial analyses and cash flows are based on grid-connected solar systems only, as opposed to self-contained systems using batteries for back-up power when the sun is not generating power through the PV panels. Most people remain tied to the grid without battery back-up, with cost being the primary reason. Batteries are expensive, and need to be replaced over time. The previous cash flow charts would reflect different cash flows and investment returns if batteries were factored in. You need to weigh the advantages of batteries against the upfront and replacement costs. If you will be using a fair amount of electricity at night and need uninterrupted service during dark days, batteries may be the best way to go.

If the Grid Goes Down, Your System Goes Down with It

Some systems have both grid connections and batteries as a backup. However, if the grid goes out due to downed power lines, blackouts, etc., you will **not** be able to run off your battery backup if you remain connected to the grid.

Many people believe that solar power gives them true energy independence, in every sense of the word. However, this can really only happen if you are completely off grid. The truth is, if the grid goes down and your solar system is tied into it, your solar power goes down with it. Why? One explanation is for safety reasons. When power goes out there are power line workers up on the lines making repairs. Solar systems generating electricity while remaining tied to the grid may cause risks for the line workers. It is not as simple as flipping a switch from grid tied to battery only. Most electrical codes do not allow this. You should check with your local utility and building codes before making your solar investment.

Keeping Up With A Changing Industry

The solar industry is in a perpetual state of change and innovation, and as such, the pros and cons of solar are subject to change as well. The preceding pages present a good guideline to determine the feasibility of a solar project for home or business. When the efficiency and technology changes, you can always plug in the new information (rated power output, cost, required maintenance, electrical storage technology, etc.) using the preceding charts as a guideline.

It's All Connected

One theme which I cannot overstate is the dynamic interaction between natural systems, technology, and building designs. The goal is to create as much synergy and balance between these systems as possible. This is particularly true when considering solar. Too much or too little shading, for example, can have a huge impact on energy usage. A well positioned tree or shading louvers, etc. could be used in lieu of all or some solar panels if the goal is to reduce overall electric costs. Don't get caught up in all the hype about solar or anything else, without first looking at the entire picture and the interrelationships that exist for your location/situation.

Respect for All Life

We are in the last quarter of 2023, and the world has gone mad. There is a total inversion of reality, where truth, common sense, and logic have been replaced by lies, talking points, and propaganda in the mainstream media. These narratives alter perceptions, which leads to decision-making and reactions to situations based on emotion and fear—the hive mind, mob mentality. Then, the old divide and conquer playbook is used to create more division and animosity among the population. Whether you are Arabic, Jewish, white, black, indigenous, Hispanic, gay, Muslim, trans... you are compartmentalized as such. This is your new limited identity—an illusion of separateness, us vs. them, creating a breeding ground of contempt and fear. Then the labels come out, further fomenting anger—antisemite, white supremacist, homophobe, republican, democrat, racist, anti-vaxer, conspiracy theorist, transphobe.... One or most of these groups are your new enemies, and all that is needed is an event such as the Israeli bombing of Gaza to set off a firestorm of animosity and bloodlust. YOUR'RE BEING PLAYED!

What I feel is an antidote to this nonsense is to respect ALL life. Period. That includes your own self-respect, and all living things, which includes all human beings, animals, plants, trees oceans, rivers, lakes.... It's all alive, all conscious, and all connected, as meticulously described in previous chapters. In addition to your personal gain from this, it creates an overall energetic shift from dense, low frequencies, to a higher frequency, a frequency which transcends low vibrational and destructive energy.

What are your belief systems? If you set the bar high enough to include the welfare of all life, you are called "unrealistic." They will say, are you crazy? We **have** to swim in contaminated water. It's just the way it is. Your utility bills will continue to rise, so just get over it. These things are too expensive to fix. Joseph Goebbels, propaganda minister of the Nazi regime said, "If you tell a lie big enough and keep repeating it, people will eventually come to believe it."

Rather than argue or debate the issue (most peoples' minds are already made up anyway) you can lead by example—literally in your own back yard. No more waiting for environmental laws to better regulate a broken system. No more "accepting" beach closures and declining water front property values due to sewage overflow and algae overgrowth. If something works and the benefits (financial, environmental, health) are big enough, other individuals, companies, and municipalities will most probably follow suit—possibly even improving upon the original idea.

As stated earlier, change of this nature will most likely occur from the bottom up—like most peaceful revolutions. This is not "green," but more of a common sense revolution, for the benefit of "all life."

Are you a creative individual, or a blind follower? Will you leave your children and grandchildren a land used up, and barely habitable, or one that is regenerating, life-enhancing, and self-sustaining?

United Nations Agenda 21/2030: Sustainable Development

Agenda 21 (recently updated and now called Agenda 2030) was allegedly designed by the United Nations to reduce man's destructive impact on the world—to reduce or eliminate land use and building practices that are "unsustainable and unhealthy" for man and all life on the planet. It was designed to reduce urban sprawl, automobile dependence; to create more protected open space and wildlife zones; to promote and build more mixed-use, high-density developments closer to urban centers with extensive light rail, bike paths; to ensure availability and sustainable management of water and sanitation; to take urgent actions to combat climate change and its impacts, etc.

This all sounds great, but at what cost? Not surprisingly, individual freedoms may/will be compromised. There may/will be more centralized control over food, water, housing, and land ownership in order to make this agenda a reality. The framers of this "New World Order" are essentially saying they don't trust the people to come up with their own solutions. Is that the real reason for this proposed massive shift in world politics? Or were these problems created by the very people who want more power and control and are using the environment as a pretext to gain that control?

It is beyond the scope of this book to fully research that question. However, you have to wonder why our current environmental, energy, health problems and other issues are not really being solved. Why are proven solutions (some of which are outlined in this book) not being implemented? Why do we have to wait for a problem to get so big that only a major political shift could solve a problem so large—a political shift that erodes freedoms and self reliance?

Maybe we have to look a little deeper as to the lack of any substantive change. There are still wars, terrorism, corruption, rampant disease, and escalated violence, but we **do** have smart phones. As the rock band The Police used to sing, "There are no political solutions.." Still, Agenda 21/2030 is hell bent on "solving problems" with even more political intervention.

Hopefully some of the solutions outlined in this book will be utilized, expanded upon, and become ever more part of the mainstream culture, thus negating the need for more centralized control in the name of sustainability. Maybe in so doing we can come to terms with our place in the natural world, and be at peace with it. Native American Chief Seattle so aptly stated:

> Humankind has not woven the web of life. We are but one thread within it. Whatever we do to the web, we do to ourselves. All things are bound together. All things connect. We are a part of the earth and it is part of us.

About The Author

Don Kulak is publisher and editor of White Pine—The Sustainable Real Estate Journal, and owns a property management company, specializing in sustainable, regenerative designs. He also worked as a real estate appraiser and served on the Georgia Lakes Society's Board of Directors.

Having attended numerous land planning and zoning board meetings, he saw grossly inefficient and expensive proposals and designs being passed on as practical solutions—with no questions asked. Through extensive research and countless interviews, he saw there were better ways to manage land, water, and the built environment using a more symbiotic approach

He believes any real positive change has to come from the bottom up—where people involved with real estate on any level can implement profitable, cost-cutting solutions while working in concert with the natural landscape. He wrote this book to help individuals become more self-reliant, and less dependent on inefficient and dirty systems that do not work in their best interests.

Prior to real estate, he founded and managed two music trade Associations: The Independent Music Association, and the Independent Music Retailers Association, and created symbiotic marketing campaigns and joint ventures between member companies for more leverage, exposure, and market share. He wrote and published Marketing Strategies for Independent Record Labels: A Guide To Effective Distribution. and edited and published Soundtrack—The Independent Music Association Journal. He initiated and won a lawsuit on behalf of his retailer members who were victims of price discrimination by four major music distributors.

Bibliography

AMEC Earth and Environmental Center for Watershed Protection. *Georgia Stormwater Management Manual, Volume 2*. Atlanta: Atlanta Regional Commission, 2001.

Barber, David. *Modern Architecture and Climate: Design Before Air Conditioning*. Princeton, New Jersey: Princeton University Press, 2020

Berry, Thomas. *The Great Work*. New York: Bell Tower Press, 1999.

Bolte-Taylor, Jill. *My Stroke of Insight*. New York: The Penguin Group, 2006.

Brenneissen, Stephan. *From Pilot to Mainstream: Green Roofs in Basel Switzerland*. Presented at the Sixth International Greening Rooftops for Sustainable Communities Conference. Basel, Switzerland, 2008.

Brown, Joseph *The Spiritual Legacy of the American Indian*. Wallingford: Pendle Hill, 1964.

Bunzel, Ruth. *Introduction to Zuñi Ceremonialism*. from the 47th Annual Report of the Bureau of American Ethnology, Washington D.C. : Smithsonian Institute, 1929.

Burdon, Peter, ed. *Exploring Wild Law – The Philosophy of Earth Jurisprudence*. South Australia: Wakefield Press, 2011.

Cavanaugh, Laura. *Green Roofs: The Durability-Sustainability Link*. Facilitiesnet. *2008*

Cohen, Jeffrey, Richard Field, Anthony Tafuri, and Michael Ports. *Cost Comparison of Conventional Grey Combined Sewer Overflow Control Infrastructure versus a Green/Gray Combination*. Reston: Journal of Irrigation and Drainage Engineering, June, 2012.

Cotterell, Janet, and Adam Dadeby. *The Passivehous Handbook*. Devon, England: Green Books, 2012.

Dubos, R. *Environmental Determinants of Human Life*. New York:

Rockefeller University Press, 1968

Duncan, Richard. Technical Director. Spray Polyurethane Foam Alliance. Interview, 2016.

Dubos, Rene. *So Human an Animal: How We are Shaped by Surroundings and Events.* United Kingdom. Taylor and Francis, 1968

Dunnett, Nigel. *Rain Gardens – Managing Water Sustainability in the Garden and Designed Landscape.* Portland: Timber Press, 2007.

EPA report 841-F-07-006. December, 2007.

Evidence from Property Sales in the Mississippi Headwaters Region. Minnesota: The Mississippi Headwaters Board and Bemidji State University, (2003).

Frago, Charlie. *Storm Leaves Bay with Sewage Mess.* Tampa Bay Times, September 7, 2016.

Freudenberger, Dean. *Agricultural Agenda for the 21st Century.* Tel Aviv, Israel: Israel Journal of Development, 1988.

Gates, Jeff. *Ownership Solution: Toward A Shared Capitalism For The 21st Century.* Jackson: Perseus Books, 1998.

Geauga Soil and Water Conservation District, *Rain Garden Design and Construction.* Fairfax, VA: The Northern Virginia Soil and Water Conservation District, 2009

Gross, E.M. *Allelopathy of Aquatic Autotrophs.* Konstanz: Limnolgical Institute, 2003.

Gupta, Plyush, Surendra Roy, and Amit Mahindrakar. *Treatment of Water Using Water Hyacinth, Water Lettuce and Vetiver Grass – A Review.* Kolar Gold Fields, India: National Institute of Rock Mechanics, 2012.

Hairston, Nelson, and Gregor Fussmann. "Lake Ecosystems." *Encyclopedia of Life Sciences.* MacMillan Publishers, 2002.

Harwood, Corbin. *Using Land to Save Energy.* Cambridge, MA: Ballinger Publishing Company, 1977.

Hemenway, Toby. *Gaia's Garden: A Guide to Home-Scale Permaculture.* White River Junction: Chelsea Green Press, 2001.

Hugel, Craig. *Native Plant Landscaping.* Gainesville: University

Press of Florida, 2010.

Icke, David. *The Perception Deception.* Isle of Wight: David Icke Books, 2013.

Johansen, Bruce. *The Iroquois.* New York: Chelsea House Publishing, 2010.

Koire, Rosa. *Behind The Green Mask: U.N. Agenda 21.* Santa Rosa: The Post Sustainable Institute Press, 2011.

Kraus, Helen, and Anne Spafford. *Rain Gardening in the South: Ecologically Designed Gardens for Drought, Deluge and Everything in Between.* Hillsborough, NC: Eno Publishers, 2010.

Krean, Patrick, and Penny Krone. *Peace: A Dream Unfolding.* Somerville: Somerville House Books, 1986.

Krysel, Charles, Elizabeth Boyer, Charles Parson, PhD., and Patrick Welle, PhD. *Lakeshore Property Values and Water Quality.* Mississippi Headwaters Board and Bemidji State University (May14, 2003)

Lampert, Winfried, and Ulrich Sommer. *Limnoecology – The Ecology of Lakes and Streams.* New York: Oxford University Press, 2007.

Leggett, Christopher G., and Nancy Bockstae. *Evidence of the Effects of Water Quality on Residential Land Prices.* College Park: Department of Agricultural and Resource Economics, University of Maryland, 1999.

Levy, Phillip A. "Iroquois Influence Thesis" William and Mary Quarterly, (July 1996).

Linzey, Thomas, and Anneke Campbell. *Be the Change.* Layton, UT: Gibbs Smith Publishing, 2009.

Lyle, John. *Regenerative Design for Sustainable Development.* Hoboken, New Jersey: Wiley Publishers, 1996

Manu, Mitra, *Nikola Tesla's Free Electricity Electronic Circuit.* Bridgeport, Connecticut: Journal of Electronic and Communication. Vol. 1, Issue No. 1, 2018

Maplight. *Federal Lobbying Database. Berkeley, CA*: Maplight.org, 2015.

Marohn, Charles. *Strong Towns.* Hoboken, New Jersey: John Wiley and Sons. 2020

McCullough, Lisa. *Conversations With Paolo Soleri*. Princeton: Princeton Architectural Press, 2012.

McNickle, D'Arcy. *They Came Here First – The Epic of American Indians*. Philadelphia, PA: J.P. Lippincott Company,1949.

Meerow, A.W, and R.J. Black. *Enviroscaping to Conserve Energy: Determining Shade Patterns for Central Florida*. Gainsville: University of Florida, 1993.

Michael, Holly J., Kevin Boyle, and Roy Bouchard, *Water Quality Affects Property Prices: A Case Study of Selected Maine Lakes.* Maine: Maine Agricultural Forest and Experiment Station, University of Maine, (1996)

Miracles of Kaethe Seidel Essay, 1990.

Sahtouris, Elisabeth. *Beautiful Bulrushes, Remarkable Reeds The Water Reclamation Miracles of Kaethe Seidel Essay*, 1990

Sanders, Mathew and Vivian Hughes. *Race to the Bottom (of the Well): Groundwater in an Agricultural Production Treadmill.* Oxford, England 2018

Sharma, Raghav. *Green Courts in India: Strengthening Environmental Governance.* Jodhpu, India: Law Environment and Development Journal, Vol. 4, No. 1, 2008.

Shepard, Paul. *Coming Home to the Pleistocene.* Edited by Florence Shepard. Washington, DC: Island Press, 1998.

Simpson, James, and Gregory McPherson. "Potential of Tree Shade for Reducing Residential Energy Use in California." *Journal of Aboriculture,* January, 1996.

Stamets, Paul. *Mycellium Running.* Berkeley: 10 Speed Press, 2005.

Stoeckelar, Joseph, and Ross Williams. *Windbreaks and Shelterbelts.* Washington D.C: Yearbook of Agriculture, 1949.

Strauss, Levi. *The Savage Mind.* Chicago: University of Chicago Press,1966.

Suzuki, David. *The Sacred Balance.* Amherst: Prometheus Books, 1998.

Tilder, Lisa, and Blostein, Beth, eds. *Design Ecologies – Essays on the*

Nature of Design. Princeton: Princeton Architectural Press, 2008.

Tillman, John. *Regenerative Design for Sustainable Development*. Hoboken: Wiley Professional, 1996.

United States General Services Administration. *The Benefits and Challenges of Green Roofs on Public and Commercial Buildings.* Washington *D.C. GSA, 2011.*

Mollison,Bill. *Permaculture – A Designers Manual.* Australia: Tagari Publications, 1988.

NAHB Research Center. *Fixture Flow Rate Comparison Cross-Linked Polyethylene (PEX) Piping and Copper Tubing.* MD, 2008

National Renewable Energy Laboratory. *U.S. Photovoltaic Prices and Cost Breakdowns.* Technical Report TP-6A20-64746, 2015

Neel, J.V. "Lessons From A Primitive People." *Science.* November, 1970. p815-822.

Nelson, Richard. *Make Prayers for the Raven A KoyukanView of the Northern Forest.* Chicago: Chicago University Press, 1986.

Office of Water Programs, California State University. *Ammonia Removal in Wetlands: a Literature Review Office of Water Programs,* Sacramento: Regional County Sanitation District, 2009.

Olgyay, Victor. *Design With Climate – Bioclimatic Approach to Architectural Regionalism.* Princeton, NJ: Princeton University Press, 1963.

Orr, David. *The Nature of Design.* Oxford, U.K.: Oxford University Press, 2002.

Pahl, Greg. *Power From the People.* White River Junction: Chelsea Green Publishing, 2012.

Payne, Samuel. *The Iroquois League, the Articles of Confederation, and The Constitution.* William and Mary Quarterly. July 1996

Robinette, Gary. *Energy Efficient Site Design.* New York: Van Nostrand and Company, 1983.

Sahtouris, Elisabet. *Beautiful Bulrushes, Remarkable Reeds The Water Reclamation Miracles of Kaethe Seidel.* 1990.

US Army Corps of Engineers Division. *Feasibility Report and Environmental Assessment Marsh Lake Ecosystem Restoration Project.*

Mississippi Valley: 2011.

Vymazal, J. *Constructed Wetlands For Wastewater Treatment – A Review*. Dukelska 145, 37901 Trebon, Czech Republic: ENKI o.p.s. and Institute of System Biology and Ecology, Czech Academy of Sciences.

Weiler, Susan, and Katrin Scholz-Barth. *Green Roof Systems : A Guide to the Planning, Design and Construction of Building Over Structure*. Hoboken: John Wiley and Sons, 2009.

Wells, Malcolm. *How to Build an Underground House.* Topeka, KS: Ogden Publications, 2009.

Werthmann, Christian. *Green Roof – A Case Study*. Princeton: Princeton Architectural Press, 2007.

Westra, Laura, Klaus Basselmann, and Richard Westra, eds. *Reconciling Human Existence With Ecological Integrity*. London: Earthscan, 2008.

Wiehagen, J., and J. L. Sikora. *Performance Comparison of Residential Hot Water Systems,* Upper Marlboro: NAHB Research Center, 2003.

Wohlleben, Peter. *The Hidden Life of Trees: What They Feel, How They Communicate – Discoveries from a Secret World. Vancouver, B. C.* Canada: Greystone Books, 2016

Wolff, Gary and Eric Hallstein. *Beyond Privatization – Restructuring Water Systems to Improve Performance.* Oakland, CA: Pacific Institute, 2005.

Woodruff, N.P. *Shelterbelt and Surface Barrier Effects on Wind Velocities, Evaporation, House Heating, and Snow Drifting.* Technical Bulletin 131. Manhattan, KS: Kansas State University of Agriculture and Applied Science, 1954.

Zinn, Howard. *Peoples History of the United States.* New York: Harper Perennial, 2003.

www.ingramcontent.com/pod-product-compliance
Lightning Source LLC
Chambersburg PA
CBHW051538020426
42333CB00016B/1989
* 9 7 8 1 7 3 5 3 5 0 0 2 8 *